THE EVERYDAY SPACE TRAVELER

Discover 9 Life-Affirming Insights into the Wonders of Inner and Outer Space

JASON KLASSI

SPACE TRAVELER PUBLISHING
LOS ANGELES, CALIFORNIA

NOTE TO THE READER: The gold figures in the glyphs in each chapter represent our body position relative *to* Earth on each leg of our journey *from* Earth. The iconic space traveler depicts the physical essence of each chapter—floating weightless, embracing mystery, rediscovering home, etc. The figure in each symbolic pictogram is a graphic expression of what legendary Russian acting coach Michael Chekhov called a "psychological gesture"—a physical body position that conjures up a certain emotional impulse.

Library of Congress Control Number: 2009914179

Klassi, Jason.

The everyday space traveler : discover 9 life-affirming insights into the wonders of inner and outer space / Jason Klassi. -- Los Angeles, Calif. : Space Traveler Pub., c2012.
         p. ; cm.

    ISBN: 978-0-9817674-0-6
    Includes bibliographical references and index.

   1. Space tourism. 2. Space flight to Mars. 3. Space flights. 4. Space travelers. 5. Outer space--Exploration. 6. Self-actualization (Psychology) 7. Interplanetary voyages. 8. Voyages, Imaginary. I. Title.

    TL793 .K53 2012   2009914179
    629.45--dc22   1201

Printed in China.
Text design by Dotti Albertine

Scan this QR code with your SmartPhone and go directly to the SpaceTraveler website.

To my family, friends
and fellow travelers on this
amazing journey of life

Contents

Foreword by Buzz Aldrin

Apollo 11 astronaut, global statesman for space, and moonwalker

WHEN I SET FOOT ON THE MOON with Apollo 11 Commander Neil Armstrong over 40 years ago, my life changed forever. Walking on the Moon taught me a lot about walking on Earth and how to live my life to the fullest on this amazing planet of ours.

Today, my mission is to make space travel affordable to everyone so that you too can benefit from the insights of space travelers. In the next few years, more and more of you will travel to space, floating weightless on board safe and comfortable spacecraft where you will experience spectacular views of Earth from orbit. This act of traveling in space will create profound changes in your life, as it did mine.

People who travel to space will come to take for granted important insights that have taken those on Earth thousands of years to formulate. *The Everyday Space Traveler* is the first book that brings space travel down to Earth and makes these profound insights available to us all. *The Everyday Space Traveler* is a book for everyone and a book whose time has come.

I've had my awesome space adventure. Now I'm working so that you too can experience the wonders of space travel—from the Moon to Mars and beyond.

Ad astra (to the stars),

Buzz

Let me say, as I sit here before you today having walked on the Moon, that I am myself still awed by that miracle. That awe, in me and in each of us... must be the engine of future achievement, not a slow dimming light from a time once bright.

―――

BUZZ ALDRIN, astronaut (1930 –)

The frozen Shellrock River in winter. The ice can be very thick and safe to walk on. But, as I discovered, there are places thin enough for a human to fall through into a swift-moving current of water; the same liquid that supports life can also easily take life away. (Figure 2) Shellrock Winter. Space Traveler, Inc.

Preface

I ALMOST DROWNED WHEN I WAS A BOY. One crispy cold, star-filled night, I was walking on the frozen Shellrock River winding through the snowy fields of Iowa.

Crack! The ice broke under my feet.

Suddenly, the frigid current pulled me deep into murky darkness. In an instant, I came so close to death that I became keenly aware of being alive.

Instead of sinking toward my death on the bottom of that dark riverbed, I fought for my life and swam as hard as I could up toward the stars twinkling through the hole in the ice. Those precious few seconds changed my life forever. That experience was a turning point in my childhood, a profound moment in my life—a *lifepoint*.

Since then, I've come to realize that I was more than just a boy drowning in a little river on a lonely planet—I was a space traveler on Earth floating among the stars, lucky to be on a mysterious cosmic voyage called life. I didn't have a near-death experience, as some people claim. I had a near-space experience.

Whenever I recall that moment, when the current swept me under the ice and away from that starlit hole, I realize how the decision to live applies not only to me but also to the rest of us. Sink... or swim!

Either life goes forward
or it goes back.
Beware the concussion.
Is it that or this?
All the Universe—
or nothingness?
Which shall it be?
Which shall it be?

———

H.G. WELLS, WRITER (1866 – 1946)

We're quickly approaching similar lifepoints in our collective future—moments in time that determine whether we survive or perish. Every day we are confronted with climate change, threats of terrorist attacks, catastrophic natural disasters and countless, needless deaths from famine, disease and poverty.

Yet, we also live in a time of unprecedented possibilities. Every day new discoveries are helping each of us live longer, healthier and happier. The benefits of space exploration can be found in everything from cell phones, to medicines, to inspiring stories.

Many of us from all walks of life want to space-travel. We have dreamed of these journeys while enjoying space-themed movies, TV programs and books. Space travel is compelling, whether it's the desire to have a life-changing view of Earth from orbit or to float weightless in space as in our flying dreams.

Polls show that over half of us would like to travel in space. The list includes celebrities such as actor Tom Hanks, movie director James Cameron and renowned physics professor Stephen Hawking; as well as everyone from high school teachers to starry-eyed children, to me and maybe you too.

Advances in private space travel, once the domain of a privileged few, are making it possible for everyday people to have the profound experience of space flight. Armchair astronauts can finally live the dream on board passenger spacecraft built by **Virgin Airlines** founder Richard Branson and Burt Rutan, the designer of history-making *SpaceShipOne*. **Virgin Galactic's** passenger spacecraft can carry six people to the edge of space where they float weightless and view the awesome Earth below.

Other prominent millionaires investing some of their fortunes in private space travel include Jeff Bezos, founder of **Amazon.com.** This successful book entrepreneur is developing a spacecraft that flies like those envisioned in early science fiction novels. Robert Bigelow, founder of the **Budget Suites** hotel chain, is test-flying inflatable cabin modules for a future space hotel.

If you are alive today, you have a very real opportunity of traveling to space before you die. Whether you personally fly to space or not, private space travel will have a tremendous effect on all our lives. We are entering a new space age. We are all participants in the dawning of a space-traveler society here on Earth.

My purpose in writing this book is to take you on a voyage into the very real world of private space travel. This book is our ship and each chapter a leg of our journey. Welcome aboard the *CosmicSea* on the world's first adventure vacation to Mars!

Astronaut Bruce McCandless II is photographed farther away from the confines
and safety of his ship than any previous astronaut has ever been. On February 12,
1984, with the aid of a jet-propelled backpack called the Manned Maneuvering
Unit (MMU), McCandless went "free-flying" to a distance of 320 feet away from the
orbiter—all alone against the blue of Earth and the vast blackness of space.

(FIGURE 3) EVATION. NASA

Introduction | Why Go?

PEOPLE WHO TRAVEL TO SPACE quickly gain important insights that have taken those on Earth thousands of years to formulate. The insights in this book are derived from real astronauts through their experiences of orbiting Earth and walking on the Moon.

These folks are not much different from you and me, except that they have left their home planet and traveled in outer space—the soul of the universe, the great cosmic sea. The experiences of astronauts are also part of our everyday lives, infused in the underlying principles of science, art, philosophy and love.

We are all born into this universe, where we live each and every day within its laws and principles. From the inescapable force of gravity throughout the universe to the bonds between the tiniest atoms in our bodies, our lives are immersed in the laws of nature. It is only natural for us to wonder about the world around us.

THE ULTIMATE ADVENTURE

Space is romantic, dramatic, beautiful, mysterious, hostile, exotic and erotic all at the same time. It has been called everything from the "edge of heaven" to the "new frontier" to the "inverted sea."

The benefits from exploring space touch our lives every day. Space travel has given us everything from the inspiration of watching humans first set foot on the Moon to the life-enhancing technologies in our hospitals and homes. Where would we be without orbiting

The hundreds of people who have flown in space substantiate one premise:

The act of traveling in space can create profound changes in a person's life.

This billowing tower of cold gas and dust rises from a stellar nursery called the Eagle Nebula. The soaring tower is 9.5 light-years or about 56 trillion miles high, about twice the distance from our Sun to the next nearest star. (FIGURE 4) STELLAR SPIRE. NASA, ESA AND THE HUBBLE HERITAGE TEAM (STScI/ AURA)

satellites that transmit our phone calls to loved ones, guide the airplanes we fly and warn us of killer hurricanes before they strike?

Space captivates our highest romantic notions whether we travel there or not. The compelling romance of space travel may lie in the very words "space" and "travel," which evoke images with a "female" and "male" sense. It's easy and understandable to see rocket ships as phallic symbols propelling the seeds of life into the vast, orb-filled womb of all creation.

Space affects us emotionally, spiritually and physically. As the Moon's gravity affects the tides of the ocean, so it affects the flow of our body fluids, hormones, emotions and reproductive urges. The Moon and planets literally move us to love, procreate and populate new worlds and distant shores.

Space is the grand environment we live in. Understanding how to exist in space has been life's quest from day one. From the very beginning of human understanding, we've been asking ourselves in grunts, groans and grandiose prose, "Why are we here? What is out there?"

PRIVATE SPACE TRAVEL

If someone had told your great-great-grandfather back in 1904—when the Wright Brothers took their short but historic flight—that within a decade a passenger airline service would be operating in America, he probably would have laughed—along with the rest of the world. Today, thanks to the Wright Brothers and others, the everyday person can take an afternoon suborbital flight to the edge of space or go all the way to orbit and circle the entire planet every ninety minutes while floating weightless.

I love space!

———

DENNIS TITO, the first private space traveler
(1940 –)

Dennis Tito, the first paying space tourist, is all smiles as he boards the International Space Station on April 30, 2001. A little stiff and cautious in the roomy station, he reported he was adapting well and proclaimed, "I love space."
(FIGURE 5) TITO. ITAR-TASS

Here we see *SpaceShipOne* nestled safely beneath her mothership, the *White Knight*.
(Figure 6) *SpaceShipOne* and *White Knight*. Mojave Aerospace Ventures, LLC.

On June 21, 2004, headlines around the world read **SpaceShipOne Makes History: First Private Manned Mission to Space.** On this historic day, everyone witnessed the dawn of a new space age as investor and philanthropist Paul G. Allen and Burt Rutan's Scaled Composites launched the first privately manned vehicle beyond Earth's atmosphere. The successful launch of *SpaceShipOne* demonstrated that the final frontier is now open to private enterprise.

We are participants in a brand-new civilization—the space-traveler society. The stage is set for an expedition like the one on which we will soon embark in this book.

SpaceShipOne at the apex
of its historic flight
(FIGURE 7) *SPACESHIPONE* APEX.
MOJAVE AEROSPACE VENTURES, LLC.

SpaceShipOne lands.
(FIGURE 8) *SPACESHIPONE* RETURNS
TO EARTH. MOJAVE AEROSPACE
VENTURES, LLC.

Everyday Travel Tip
OPEN A SPACE VACATION INVESTMENT ACCOUNT

Let the power of compound interest help you reach your weightless destination in space and other destinations on your journey through life.

Pay off all your high-interest credit card debt first, if you have any. Then invest as much of your annual income as you can to your space vacation account in addition to your other savings accounts. Over time, the power of compounding interest can make money grow geometrically.

Common sense says: Do more with less and invest the rest every day. When there's a space vacation package right for you, you'll be ready to go.

Astronaut Mike Mullane on board the Space Shuttle enjoying the pleasurable pastime of taking pictures of his home planet, Earth

(FIGURE 9) MIKE MULLANE. NASA/JOHNSON SPACE CENTER

I think all of us know in our souls that the richest we have ever been is when we were 200 miles above Earth looking down. No earthly wealth will ever compare to that. You will come to know that too. Which is why all people who want to go, need to go. It's imperative to our continued evolution.

——

MIKE MULLANE, Space Shuttle mission specialist (1945 –)

OUR VIRTUAL JOURNEY

We've all heard the metaphor "life is a journey." And since a metaphor is a comparison of truths, then "life is a space journey" could be one of the ultimate metaphors in the poetry of our lives.

As famed author Ray Bradbury said, "Science fiction pretends to look into the future, but it's really looking at a reflection of the truth immediately in front of us." Truth, or seeing things as they really are, is fundamental to everyone's survival. Envisioning truthful, realistic scenarios is a basic survival tool.

What would it be like to travel aboard a spaceyacht of the not-too-distant future designed to take six people on the world's first televised adventure to Mars? What if we could take a space vacation like the journey described in the following travel brochure? **What if one of those space travelers were you?**

The point of this book's scenario is not to foretell the future but to explore the possibilities. On this journey, we will see how the truths of space travelers can shed insight into our everyday lives. By stepping into the future in our minds, we may make better use of the present.

Prediction is very difficult, especially about the future.

———

Niels Bohr, physicist (1885 – 1962)

EXPEDiTiON LiFEPOiNT

Departure Date

July 4, 2099

Join a select group of everyday people on one of humankind's greatest quests—THE SEARCH FOR LIFE ON ANOTHER PLANET—and discover new insights into your own life.

Expedition LifePoint—the space-adventure vacation brochure

(FIGURE 10) EXPEDITION LIFEPOINT. SPACE TRAVELER, INC.

EXPEDITION LIFEPOINT is the world's first adventure vacation to **Mars**—and an unprecedented television event. You and your shipmates will cruise to New Shangri-la, the first small but thriving human colony on another planet. You'll travel aboard *CosmicSea*, an expedition-class spaceyacht, on a journey that will change your life and the lives of everyone watching back home on Earth.

People around the world watch members of Expedition LifePoint search for life on the surface of Mars. (FIGURE 11) VIDEOTRON. SPACE TRAVELER, INC.

We depart on **EXPEDITION LIFEPOINT** aboard our spaceyacht *CosmicSea*.

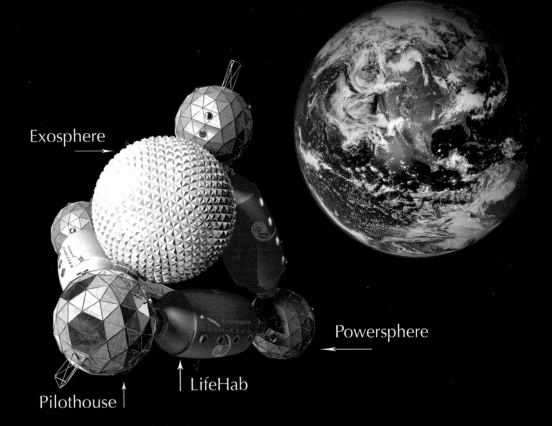

Exosphere

Powersphere

LifeHab

Pilothouse

CosmicSea is a comfortable and capable spaceship with all the amenities of a fine ocean-going yacht. Even the portholes in our private cabins are nautically framed with glistening composite metals resembling bronze and wood. Outside our windows we can see our home planet, Earth; our destination, Mars; and a universe full of stars.

CosmicSea departs Earth on its way to Mars. The gold Pilothouse at the nose of the craft is comparable to the helm of a ship. Directly behind the Pilothouse are the GalleyHab and the CabinHab, where we'll eat and sleep. The two UtilityHabs above deck are for supplies and life-support systems. The three silver Powerspheres house the engines. The Exosphere, a miniature biosphere of Earth, is where we supplement our water and oxygen supply, grow fresh food to complement our daily meals and enjoy ample room for weightless recreation.

(FIGURE 12) *COSMICSEA* DEPARTS. SPACE TRAVELER, INC.

During this cruise, we'll enjoy space exploration and zero-gravity living at its finest.

After landing on Mars, we'll join 12 other brave pioneers looking for signs of life beyond Earth. Tiny, discreet cameras embedded in our clothing, tools and vehicles will transmit our exciting discoveries to viewers back on Earth. Although the robotic eyes of unmanned spacecraft can tell us a great deal about the composition of other planets, it may take a human being with intelligence, insight and intuition to find life in the Red Planet's hidden realms.

CosmicSea's spacious accommodations are ideal for weightless recreation and relaxation.

(FIGURE 13) WEIGHTLESS. SPACE TRAVELER, INC.

If you're looking for something more from your next vacation, join **EXPEDİTİON LİFEPOİNT.** Change your life and the lives of everyone back home on Earth.

WELCOME ABOARD!
Your Captain,
Spacejace
May 28, 2098

Residents of the New Shangri-la Mars Base will greet us upon our arrival.

(Figure 14) Mars Explorers. NASA/JSC by Pat Rowlings

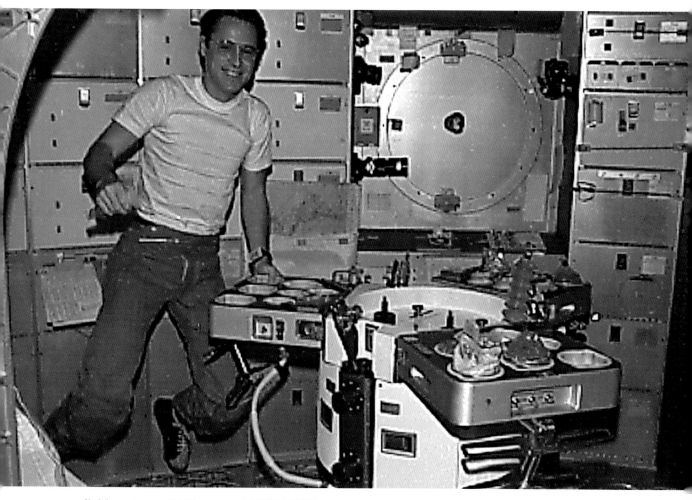

Skylab-4 astronaut Ed Gibson, seen here preparing a meal, believes that the more people who experience space, the greater difference it will make for all of us.
(Figure 15) Ed Gibson. NASA/ Marshall Space Flight Center

LIFEPOINT

Why go on a journey such as Expedition LifePoint? As with most journeys, we want to have an incredible experience somewhere unique and live to tell about it. We want to come home with great stories and a new understanding of life.

Skylab astronaut Ed Gibson believes that the more people who experience space, the greater difference it will make for all of us.[1] A televised adventure like Expedition LifePoint could give the rest of the world the vicarious adventure of a lifetime.

If such a journey did happen, how would things on Earth change? How would we all change? How would *you* change?

TIPPING POINTS

Change happens. Lots of little changes can add up to create one enormous, irreversible effect. Such geometrical progressions can be found in everything from climate change to disease epidemics, from fashion trends to hit songs, from biological evolution to technological innovation.

Many small events can reach a point of sudden, overwhelming critical mass—a tipping point, as science writer Malcolm Gladwell calls it.[2] Some experts who chart the rate of change suggest a threshold may happen around the year 2035.[3] Science philosopher Terence McKenna suggests that the tipping point or "Timewave Zero" could happen much sooner.

Accelerating change is a pattern that runs throughout human history. Significant events happen in a fraction of the time as preceding events. Take, for example, the ever-increasing power of computers. According to author Ray Kurzweil, computers will soon surpass the abilities of the human brain—at that point, computers will make better computers than humans can.

Eventually, accelerating rates of change come to a definite end, when the cycles are compressed from years, into months, into weeks, into days…into a single moment. At the rate humans are currently progressing, author Peter Russell believes it is possible that we could find ourselves evolving so fast that we experience an unimaginable degree of evolution within a finite time. We would reach a point of singularity[4]—a moment in time when only one option is possible—either we go forward or we go back.

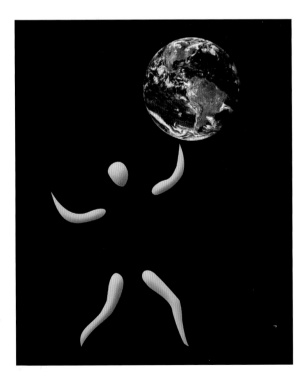

One iconic Space Traveler attempts to hold the balance of Earth in her hands.
(FIGURE 16) TIPPING POINT.
SPACE TRAVELER, INC.

LIFEPOINT OR BUST

In the late 1800s, the visionary French biologist Pierre Teilhard de Chardin foresaw an "Omega Point," when a majority of humans would emphatically realize that we are indeed critical players in the human/Earth system. Chardin believed that the Omega Point would cause a collective jump in consciousness for life on Earth; the resulting widespread compassion would create a new state of peace and planetary unity.

We are at the threshold of humanity's long-term existence in the universe. At any given moment, a worldwide disaster could threaten all life on Earth. The global tipping point could result from a sudden drastic change in our climate, the spread of a killer virus, a nuclear winter or an asteroid strike comparable to the one that killed off the dinosaurs. We may see the catastrophe coming—or the disaster may strike us broadside, where we're completely unaware until it hits.

Knowing such threats lurk in our future, journeys like Expedition LifePoint can foster hopeful options for everyone. Starting human colonies on the Moon or Mars could give birth to a new off-shoot of humanity and ensure our children's survival. Learning to live off Earth can help us live better on Earth.

On our journey to Mars, we'll explore the technology, science and insights of real space travelers and discover the deep significance of these in our lives here on Earth. These nine space-traveler insights can range from practical to philosophical, from public to personal. How you use them is up to you.

Pierre Teilhard de Chardin
(Figure 17) de Chardin.
Anonymous

Humankind reaches the precipice of LifePoint.

(FIGURE 18) LIFEPOINT CLIFF. SPACE TRAVELER, INC.

ACT I

PREPARING

I prepared excitedly for my departure,
as if this journey had a mysterious significance.

———

Nikos Kazantzakis, Greek writer (1883 – 1975)

The blue marble of Earth, featuring North and South America

(Figure 19) Blue Marble West. NASA

CHAPTER ONE

Space-Traveling Every Day

Author's Log
THE PRESENT—ON THE RIDE OF OUR LIVES

At this very moment, you and I are traveling through space!

You may be sitting down as you read this, but you and I are also spinning on Earth's surface at over 800 miles per hour.[1]

At the same time, we are circling the Sun at over 60,000 miles per hour. All the while, our solar system in the Milky Way Galaxy speeds along at hundreds of thousands of miles per hour. Even at speeds like that, it takes about 220 million years for the Sun to complete one loop around the center of our galaxy.

We already are space travelers. We space-travel aboard Earth every day. Every year on our birthday, we celebrate another orbit around the Sun.

Earth is the mothership we travel on. She is currently the only refuge for our survival. We have no evidence of any other planet anywhere—where life is so plentiful—or, for that matter, where life exists at all.

Our actions on Earth determine how well we survive, or don't survive. Every day tremendous challenges and opportunities confront each of us.

All of us are, always have been, and so long as we exist, always will be–nothing else but–astronauts. We indeed are in space.

_____

BUCKMINSTER FULLER, inventor/philosopher
(1895 – 1983)

THE MOTION OF OUR LIVES

Every day, we conduct our lives on Earth while moving rapidly through the vast environment of space. Yet, from here on Earth's surface, we sense almost no motion even though we're rotating faster than the speed of sound. Likewise, astronauts orbiting above Earth seldom sense motion though they are moving at thousands of miles an hour.

That's because *motion is always measured in relation to another object or reference point.* The closer the reference point, the more pronounced the sense of motion.

When we drive or ride in a car, the road is our reference point and the surroundings whiz past us, giving us the sensation of motion. When we fly in an airplane, Earth slowly moving beneath us is our reference point. As we stand on Earth, our closest reference point is the Moon. The inability to sense our movement through space can make us take for granted our role as space travelers.

BE AWARE OF YOUR SURROUNDINGS

Whether you're reading this book in the comfort of your home or driving your car in a lightning storm, whether you're lost in the woods or trying to find a bakery in the city, it helps to be aware of your surroundings. Where is the Sun in the sky? What is the direction of the wind? Where is the smell of freshly baked bread coming from?

Get a sense of your movement through space on the surface of this planet. Whether you're a pedestrian crossing a busy city street or a vacationer on safari in lion country, be aware of *all* that surrounds you.

In this day and age of tragic attacks by terrorists and catastrophic climatic disasters, we may suddenly need to save ourselves in a matter of seconds!

Primary Law of Survival:

The more we understand an environment and the less we try to fight it, the kinder it will be to us.

———

Richard Perron, author of *The Survival Bible* (1947 –)

A close-up view of astronaut Bruce McCandless II in the Manned Maneuvering Unit (MMU)

(Figure 20) Spacewalking MMU. NASA

THE SPACE EXPERIENCE

Nothing compares to the actual experience of being in outer space. Apollo 17 astronaut Harrison "Jack" Schmitt's biggest regret is that he couldn't have stayed longer on the Moon.

"Another day would have been nice," he said. "It's a fascinating place…but it's the sort of experience that's not readily transferable. It's like trying to describe what you feel when you're standing on the rim of the Grand Canyon or remembering your first love or the birth of your child. You have to be there to really know what it's like. Being there is an essential ingredient of the human experience."[2]

"It's the saddest moment of my life," Ed White uttered when he had to go back inside his spacecraft. White was America's first spacewalker. Those who have been on a spacewalk say there is nothing like it. There is a freedom you just don't get on Earth. (FIGURE 21) ED WHITE. NASA

How can we experience space travel without going to space? Fortunately, there are many enlightening experiences right here on Earth that can provide insight into space-traveling.

EXPERIENCING SPACE ON EARTH

Astronauts claim that the two pivotal experiences of space travel are viewing Earth from orbit and floating weightless.

Although you may not remember it, your first experience of being weightless was as an unborn child floating in your mother's womb. This primal experience is locked forever in your visceral memory bank. It's one, I believe, that we all subconsciously long to feel again.

As infants, we may have experienced those wondrous weightless moments when our mom or dad would toss us lovingly into the air. For a split second, we would hang in space, thrilled by pure weightless joy before landing safely in the warm embrace of our parents.

SWING SETS, SWIMMING POOLS AND STARS

As we grow older, we re-experience those early feelings of weightlessness by swinging on a swing. Back and forth we sway—gleefully hanging between up and down, suspended in mid-air, floating between the heavens and Earth—for a few brief but blissful moments. Then, as we swing back down toward the ground, our stomach sinks and our face skin droops as we experience the powerful force of gravity.

We can have similar weightless sensations by rocking in a hammock, riding a roller coaster or floating neutrally buoyant in a swimming pool. Floating in water is so space-like that NASA trains astronauts in large water-filled tanks with the help of scuba divers.

Next time you go swimming, imagine floating weightless. Lie back in a swimming pool at night and look up at the star-studded outer space.

This exuberant child experiences absolute joy with the momentary feeling of weightlessness induced by his dad's playful toss.

(FIGURE 22) WEIGHTLESS CHILD. © JOSEPH SOHM, VISIONSOFAMERICA.COM

ZERO-GRAVITY FLIGHTS

Another way to experience weightlessness is by flying in a specially designed aircraft that offers up to 30 seconds of free-fall during a series of parabolic flight paths. In a pattern similar to the arc of a swing, these aircraft point their nose 45 degrees up in the air, arch over and then drop 10,000 feet at 45 degrees.

With each parabolic arc through the air, we experience almost half a minute of weightlessness, or zero G. At the high points of our roller coaster ride through the sky, we float gently inside the padded fuselage, perform weightless acrobatics with our friends and fly from one end of the plane to the other like Superman. As the aircraft pulls out of the dive, we experience twice the force of gravity, or 2 Gs.

Reality check: It is not uncommon for even the heartiest of space travelers to regurgitate what they ate before their launch. That's why NASA's parabolic flight aircraft earned the nickname the "Vomit Comet."

Space is a topsy-turvy world. Sensors in your inner ear signal the brain that the familiar tug of Earth's gravity is missing. The resulting space adaptation syndrome can include vertigo, nausea, headaches and, in some cases, vomiting. Treatment with medications like Scopalamine are effective, but everything from meditation, fasting, yoga and biofeedback can also help.

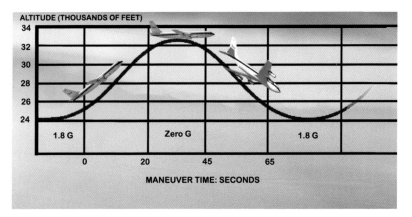

A parabolic flight path can create up to 30 seconds of weightlessness each dive.
(Figure 23) Parabolic. Space Traveler, Inc.

Randy J. Bresnik and Shannon Walker, along with other pilot candidates, enjoy "weightlessness" during a reduced-gravity session created when a KC-135 aircraft flies in a parabolic pattern.

(FIGURE 24) PARABOLIC-PLAY. NASA

Climbing a mountain is one of the few ways you can get "closer" to space without being enclosed in a pressurized airplane. This picture of Mt. Everest, the highest point on Earth, was taken from the International Space Station.

(FIGURE 25) EVEREST. NASA

MOUNTAINTOPS, AIRPLANES AND STARS

Another near-space experience can be found on high mountaintops where there is nothing but Earth's thin atmosphere separating us from the crisp breath of space. Climbing a very tall mountain is one way we can get closer to space on our own two feet. Like space, these are cold, harsh environments with little oxygen that affect us both physically and mentally.

FROM OCEANS TO SPACE

"Adventuring under the sea is an unearthly experience," wrote aquanaut William Beebe. In 1934, Beebe descended more than a half mile into the ocean off Bermuda in a steel bathysphere.

Beebe continued, "And in all except one sense we are actually entering a new world when we put on a diving helmet and float down to the white coral sand. The only other place comparable to these marvelous nether regions must surely be naked space itself, out far beyond atmosphere, between the stars, where sunlight has no grip upon the dust and rubbish of our planetary air, where the blackness of space, the shining planets, comets, suns and stars must really be closely akin to the world of life as it appears to the eyes of an awed human being in the open ocean a half mile down. **In my present existence there is only one experience left which can transcend that of living for a time under the sea—and that is a trip to Mars.**"[3]

When orbiting in the blackness of space, space travelers relish the deep blue view of the oceans that cover approximately 3/4 of Earth's surface.

Ocean travelers, on the other hand, don't simply look down at Earth from space. Seafarers are part of the planet and subject to the power of weather and waves. Alone on a vast horizon except for shipmates and the ship, all you have to do is look up into the sky to realize you're already in space.

As for the undersea world, almost anyone can experience the watery realm without even getting wet, thanks to a variety of submarines. A weekend sub-sea traveler can explore depths up to 200 feet inside a comfortable tourist submarine. The more adventurous can ride a specialized deep-diving submersible to visit the historic *Titanic* or giant pink tubeworms living next to undersea volcanoes.

For a truly enveloping near-space experience, try snorkeling or scuba diving in the deep blue vastness of the ocean surrounded by the incredible life forms of our liquid planet.

William Beebe peers out through a porthole from inside his bathysphere.
(Figure 26) Beebe. Wildlife Conservation Society

One afternoon off the coast of Hawaii, I was scuba diving with 5,000 feet of water beneath me. We were filming the installation of a large ocean energy system called OTEC, or ocean thermal energy conversion. We were hovering in deep blue liquid space with other aquanauts as they constructed this enormous energy device beneath the bottom of a ship. The underwater scene was vividly comparable to the construction of a space facility. The experience made me realize the similarities between working in the ocean and in space.

Like a spacewalking astronaut tethered to keep from floating off into the blackness of space, I felt an extreme sense of awe and helplessness at the thought of sinking into the seemingly never ending darkness beneath me. Unlike astronauts, we had to deal with three large white-tipped sharks that were more curious about man than about this man-made energy device.

Underwater installation of OTEC (ocean thermal energy conversion)
(FIGURE 27) OTEC INSTALLATION. SPACE TRAVELER, INC.

SOLAR ECLIPSES AND ANCIENT ASTRONOMERS

If you prefer to remain on terra firma, then you can experience a dazzling meteor shower, an aurora borealis or a solar eclipse. A total eclipse of the Sun is an incredible celestial experience that has astounded humans throughout time. Experiencing the ever-constant Moon block out the light of our everyday Sun is evidence of our space-traveling on Earth. A solar eclipse is a time when we are aware of being part of a larger system in space.

First Insight
SPACE TRAVELING EVERY DAY

We already are space travelers. Each of us is a crewmember on spaceship Earth—spinning at 800 miles per hour while circling the sun at more than 60,000 miles per hour. Whether we are reading this book, asleep in our homes, at work in our office or riding the subway, we are in constant motion through the universe protected only by Earth's fragile atmosphere.

Apply the primary law of survival: understand and make the most of your surroundings. You are space-traveling every moment of your life.

A view of Earth from *Genesis 2*, the second test module for Robert Bigelow's space hotel (FIGURE 28) *GENESIS 2*. BIGELOW AEROSPACE

Total solar eclipses are a geometrical coincidence. Although the Sun is 400 times larger than the Moon, it is also 400 times farther away from Earth. This makes the two bodies seem the same size when they overlap. Stand in the 150-kilometer-wide Path of Totality when the Moon passes directly in front of the Sun and you can experience night in the middle of the day.

Author's Log
JULY 11, 1991—TEOTIHUACAN, MEXICO

Here it is—the part of the solar eclipse we've all been waiting for: the Moment of Totality.

The Moon is completely covering the Sun. Only the corona's light flames flare out from behind the dark disk of the Moon.

In a matter of seconds, day becomes night. Nocturnal bats emerge in streams from nearby caves. Cars turn on their headlights. The temperature falls from midday warm to nighttime cool.

On this ancient site an hour's drive from modern Mexico City, thousands of people are standing on the Pyramid of the Sun and the Pyramid of the Moon, sharing an astonishing cosmic experience—a total solar eclipse. They are cheering, lighting candles and singing in ceremonious honor of the universe.

Three thousand years ago, Mayan priest astronomers studied the stars here and defined a thriving civilization with their profound knowledge of the solar system. Two thousand years ago, the people who lived in this astronomically designed city disappeared off the face of the earth forever. What remains of Teotihuacan is convincing evidence of a human civilization that tried to understand their place in the cosmos.

Beyond the astronomical calculations, the deeper significance of Teotihuacan's monuments to the stars lies in the beliefs and passions of the people who built them. For thousands of years, all of humanity's analytical and technological creations have been mere functional expressions of our desire to live, love and understand our place in the universe.

The citizens of Teotihuacan had a reverence for something we've come to take for granted. This ancient civilization with its celestial social structure provides the first and most fundamental insight into Expedition LifePoint: **We already are space travelers.**

But what happened to these people who appeared to understand the universe so well? How could this apparently thriving and advanced civilization become extinct? Could the same thing happen to us?

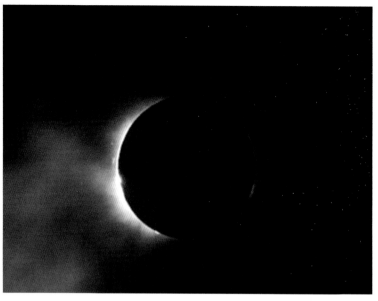

An eclipse of the Sun
(Figure 29) Eclipse. NASA

The Pyramid of the Moon only minutes before the total eclipse in 1991 at Teotihuacan, Mexico.
(Figure 30) Pyramid Moon. Space Traveler, Inc.

Apollo 12 astronaut Alan Bean

(FIGURE 31) ALAN BEAN. NASA

CHAPTER TWO

Exploring Inner Space

Author's Log
THE TIME IS NOW—WE ARE INWARD BOUND

Before we travel the endless realm of outer space, we'll first explore the equally boundless territory of our own inner space. Inner strength and self-knowledge are essential for survival on any challenging adventure, especially this one.

Our journey to Mars will make our everyday lives very different. We will be confined to our ship and limited to the monotony of the same entertainments, the same food and the same faces. We will be alone in an environment that constantly threatens us with death.

Inner calm and basic survival skills can help us thrive in outer space and on Earth. Inner peace—don't leave home without it!

What lies behind us and what lies in front of us pales in comparison to what lies within us.

———

RALPH WALDO EMERSON, writer
(1803 – 1882)

A JOURNEY OF SELF-DISCOVERY

JUDGING BY THE ACCOUNTS OF ASTRONAUTS, space travel expands human consciousness. Apollo 12 moonwalker Alan Bean became an artist upon returning to Earth. "Everybody who went to the Moon," he said, "became more like they were deep inside themselves."

Astronaut Al Worden started writing poetry after his Apollo 15 flight. Astronaut Jim Irwin returned home from the same lunar mission and said he "found God on the Moon."

— 35 —

The Thinker, superimposed in front of an image of Earth, seems to be reflecting on his place in the universe.

(FIGURE 32) THINKER. NASA AND SPACE TRAVELER, INC.

While floating in outer space, Apollo 9 astronaut Rusty Schweikart "fell in love with Earth," looked at the stars and asked soul-searching questions like, "Who am I? What is this Universe I live in?"

A few months before his famous flight in 2001, when he became the world's first space tourist, Dennis Tito and a group of us[1] went to see the movie *Space Cowboys*—an evening that Dennis credits with inspiring his final decision to fly into space. After the movie, over

Apollo 14 astronaut Edgar Mitchell with view of Earth from Apollo 13. Note: this image is a superimposition of photographs from two different Apollo missions and is not to scale. (FIGURE 33) EDGAR MITCHELL. NASA AND SPACE TRAVELER, INC.

There is only one great adventure and that is inwards towards the self.

———

HENRY MILLER, writer (1891 – 1980)

dinner, Dennis told us about the profound effect space travel had on the cosmonauts he'd met during his training in Russia's Star City. With deep conviction, he summed up their feelings; he looked at me with wide eyes and said, "It's a spiritual experience." I could tell he was looking forward to the powerful effect space travel would have on him.

OUR INWARD JOURNEY

Like space travelers, heroes and heroines of classic adventure stories are usually given **two great tasks to perform. The first is to withdraw from everyday life,** and to enter another world or explore the powerful dimensions of inner space. **The second task is to return to everyday life now armed with secret knowledge from distant domains and put it to use** in the redemption of society. For us, the second task will come soon enough on another part of our journey. Right now, we must face the first great task of heroic travelers— exploring inner space.

> **Everyday Travel Tip**
> **CREATE AND MEDITATE**
>
> Explore your inner self by engaging in an artistic endeavor like painting, music or dance. Learn to calm your mind with everything from meditation to self-hypnosis. Immerse yourself completely in nature or art.

The ability to imagine is the largest part of what you call intelligence. You think the ability to imagine is merely a useful step on the way to solving a problem and making something happen. But imagining it is what makes it happen.

———
MICHAEL CRICHTON, writer (1942 – 2008)

When astronauts began exploring outer space with rockets in the 1960s, an entire generation began exploring inner space with meditation, psychotropic drugs and other types of spiritual quests. It seems the farther out we as a species travel, the more we strive to understand our inner selves. And in doing so, we begin to understand the existence of a higher level of being.

When astronaut Edgar Mitchell went to the Moon on Apollo 14, he was "overwhelmed with a divine presence."

He experienced Earth and the universe as "an intelligent system" in a way that seemed to be at odds with his scientific training.[2]

The feeling of weightlessness and seeing Earth from space prompted Mitchell upon his return to explore consciousness and to establish the Institute of Noetic Sciences. Mitchell and his colleagues at the institute have been researching human potential for the past 25 years. These inner space explorers are studying everything from the effect of intentions on healing to expanding consciousness through meditation, biofeedback and creativity.

The creative person can take advantage of unexpected events by being open to chance and improvising with the resources at hand. Thriving in everyday life can be achieved by knowing how to survive creatively.

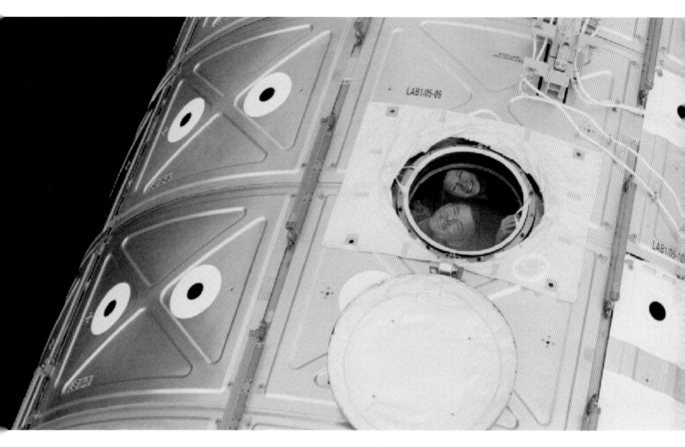

A close look at the window in this picture of the Destiny laboratory of the International Space Station reveals the faces of astronauts Susan J. Helms and James S. Voss, flight engineers for the Expedition Two mission. (FIGURE 34) HELMS-VOSS. NASA

ARE YOU A GOOD INNER SPACE TRAVELER?

As we travel outer space on Expedition LifePoint, we may discover new things about ourselves along the way—our strengths, our weaknesses.

How would you cope confined in a small spacecraft or Mars base for days, weeks, months and even years at a time with the same handful of people? Can we survive a journey to Mars without going completely crazy?

On May 20, 1898, aboard the ship *Belgica* off the coast of Antarctica, explorer Frederick Cook wrote in his log, "We are as tired of each other's company as we are of the cold monotony of the black night and of the unpalatable sameness of our food. Physically, mentally, and perhaps morally, we are depressed, and from my past experience I know that this depression will increase."

Animasphere superimposed with astronaut Susan J. Helms in the ISS.
(Figure 35) Animasphere-Helms. NASA and Space Traveler, Inc.

Because traveling in outer space requires a certain amount of inner calm, NASA and private enterprise are developing tiny computers that may one day psychoanalyze astronauts and keep them from going nuts on long space missions. If these therapist-like computers can catch depression, anxiety and other mental disorders, then perhaps it can warn of danger before it happens—in space or in schoolyards.[3]

Programmed with enough "emotion" to seem trustworthy, a space-traveling "companion computer" like *CosmicSea's* "Animasphere" could offer suggestions like, "Relax, take three deep breaths. Maybe you should take an hour out of your work schedule to rest. Let me help you with some of your daily tasks like your Author's Log."

Most of us need a little quality alone time in our daily lives. Even a few moments away from the boss, the kids or a spouse can bring us precious peace of mind. Processing our deep internal thoughts can create a clearer course of action and stronger self-confidence.

Although some quality alone time may be as necessary to life as air, water, warmth and shelter—we also need companionship. After an extremely long time alone in any environment, we might surely die of loneliness. Extreme isolation can break a person's will to live.

Survival expert Richard Perron writes, "The worst of all psychological torments is loneliness."

Who would you want for a space-travel companion?

OUR SHIPMATES

Lots of people want to space-travel. Everyone from celebrities to teachers, scientists and mega-wealthy entrepreneurs are ready to travel in space. Out of all the possible candidates, who would you like to travel with on a long-term mission like Expedition LifePoint?

Our shipmates could include a wide variety of people based on a TV show's selection criteria. For the opportunity to send a celebrity on one of the greatest media expeditions of all time, a major television network could in turn fund a qualified doctor. A group of corporate sponsors could fund the engineers who use their products on camera. A global Internet fund, for example, could back an African woman because of her knowledge of astrobiology. In

addition to our qualified captain and his crew of two, rounding out our shipmates would be you and me.

According to psychologist JoAnna Wood, an ideal Mars crew would have a range of personalities. She would want at least one person, but not more than one, who is exceptionally good at taking charge in a crisis—someone who is naturally a counselor, who takes care of other people's emotional needs. She wouldn't want everyone to be like that, however, because then they'd get nothing done.

"For Mars," she says, "everyone's got to have a sense of humor about life. The trip is going to be full of surprises, and people who have rigid expectations are not going to be any fun."[4]

THE WILL TO SURVIVE

When the Apollo 13 astronauts faced disaster and death on their return from the Moon, their calm, composure and inner strength helped saved their lives. Things were going well, like previous Apollo missions, when an oxygen tank exploded, leaving the men without power and a diminishing air supply. The world listened as the historic and understated message came crackling over the radio from the Command Module *Odyssey* almost 200,000 miles from Earth (320,000 kilometers), *"Okay, Houston, we've had a problem here...."*

The Moon and Command Module as viewed by the Apollo 13 astronauts inside the disabled Lunar Module (FIGURE 36) APOLLO 13. NASA

Everyday Travel Tip
LIGHTEN UP!

Find things in your everyday life that you can laugh at. Sometimes it helps to laugh even in moments of frustration, anguish or turmoil. Laughing is a form of deep breathing and induces a sense of inner calm.

We would surely want to share laughter with our shipmates on a long journey to Mars.

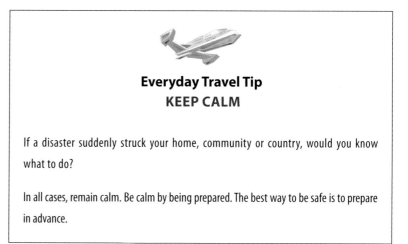

Everyday Travel Tip
KEEP CALM

If a disaster suddenly struck your home, community or country, would you know what to do?

In all cases, remain calm. Be calm by being prepared. The best way to be safe is to prepare in advance.

THE SKILLS TO SURVIVE

Disaster can sneak up on any of us at any time. Everything from a medical emergency, a house fire or an earthquake can instantly change our lives forever. When disaster strikes, can you maintain composure and take positive action?

People caught in chaos are rarely at their best. They are scared, confused and desperate for clear direction. Some people confronted with catastrophe may actually collapse in a state of panic. They become consumed by despair and ignore reality. Avoiding the truth will only make it worse. Positive action is required.

Make a plan to get in touch with your loved ones in the event of an emergency. If you survive the first 15 minutes of a major disaster, then be prepared to survive on your own for the first three days. Don't count on your neighbor, your local firemen or the National Guard to come to your rescue. It may take a governmental agency days to mobilize and get to you.

Be prepared to survive on your own or in a small group. Create a stockpile of supplies so that you can survive for at least seven days.

True *survival* is emerging from a natural or manmade disaster safely and recovering quickly. When prepared, all kinds of people can overcome seemingly impossible situations with **the right skills and the will to survive.**

No matter where we are, in our homes on Earth or in a spacecraft traveling to Mars, we can find peace of mind in being prepared for possible disaster.

Apollo 11 astronaut Buzz Aldrin on the Moon. Neil Armstrong is reflected in visor.

(FIGURE 39) BUZZ ALDRIN. NASA

When disaster strikes, keep calm, as if you are the eye of a storm.

(FIGURE 40) EYE STORM. SPACE TRAVELER, INC.

In the end, one only
experiences oneself.

———

Friedrich Nietzsche, German philosopher
(1844 – 1900)

BREATHE

In 1969, Buzz Aldrin looked forward to his famous, but almost disastrous, Apollo 11 moon landing. He later said, "We always worry. We're concerned about what can go wrong… Maybe you just breathe deeply, be as alert as possible and expect the best."[5]

Breathing deeply helps us remain calm and alert. Whether you're someone stepping into a cold shower, a mother giving birth, a runner in a marathon or a rock singer on stage, pushing all the air out of the lungs makes room for new energized air and recharges your nervous system.

Make a habit of breathing deeply throughout the day. Proper breathing can alleviate stress in true survival situations as well as in the trials of everyday life.

Three-quarters of Earth's surface is covered in water. Earth is the only water planet we know of. (Figure 41) Earth Water. NASA

Astronauts Carl J. Meade and Mark C. Lee test an EVA Rescue system some 130 nautical miles above Earth during their shared spacewalk. (FIGURE 42) SAFER RESCUE. NASA/JSC

No matter
where you go—
there you are.

———

EARL MAC RAUCH, screenwriter (1984 –)

Trained as an engineer and scientist, space traveler Edgar Mitchell was most comfortable in the realms of rationality and physical precision. Yet, having just walked on the Moon, he became convinced that **the uncharted territory of the human mind was the next frontier to explore.** As he approached his home planet, the returning astronaut was filled with an inner conviction that we are all part of a living system and we all participate in creating its collective consciousness.

Today, we don't have to be athletic astronauts or scientific geniuses to be good space travelers. However, maintaining the right attitude at such a high altitude is critical.

A sole cosmonaut looks out the window of the Russian *Mir* space station.
(FIGURE 43) FACE-IN-*MIR*. NASA

Everyday Travel Tip
MUSIC CAN BE A COMPANION

In 1947, Thor Heyerdahl led an expedition on a handmade balsa raft called *Kon-Tiki* to prove the possibility that aboriginal people could have migrated from Peru to Polynesia. During their many days adrift at sea, the men read, studied and sang songs to break the monotony of their arduous adventure.

Whether you're traveling alone in a car or with others in a spacecraft, music can help ease the pain of isolation, boredom and panic. Singing a simple song or listening to music can calm nerves and improve your outlook.

The balsa wood raft *Kon-Tiki* was built as a copy of a prehistoric South American vessel. It was constructed of nine balsa logs collected from Equador. With a crew of six men, the *Kon-Tiki* sailed from Callao in Peru on the 28th of April, 1947, and landed on the island of Raroia in Polynesia after 101 days.

(FIGURE 44) *KON-TIKI.* ANONYMOUS

Second Insight
EXPLORING INNER SPACE

Every day is a journey of self-discovery.

Before departing on any great adventure, prepare yourself physically and mentally. Being prepared for any potential disaster can help you remain calm whenever one may strike.

Remember, the first great task of the classic hero and heroine is to withdraw from everyday life and explore another world. On your heroic journey, remain calm when faced with difficult challenges. Breathe deeply and be prepared with the skills, will and inner strength to survive. Understanding your "inner space" can help you thrive in "outer space."

The Shore of Inner Space (FIGURE 45) INNER SPACE SHORE. SPACE TRAVELER, INC., AND JON KLASSI

Author's Log
PREPARING FOR OUTER SPACE WITH AN INNER-SPACE ENCOUNTER

As a child, I always dreamed of swimming with dolphins. One misty morning as a young adult, I found myself standing on the shore of Kealakekua Bay in Hawaii with my dream leaping in front of me.

Because I'd heard local islanders tell stories of the spinner dolphins that came to visit this picturesque bay every day at sunrise, I was up at dawn and ready to live my dream. Sure enough, I could soon see the acrobatic creatures coming toward me in playful, spinning leaps.

I jumped in the water and swam excitedly toward the elusive animals. Then, out of the deep blue, a large shark appeared. At first I was frightened and, I admit, I swam back to shore—quickly.

Dolphins at play in Kealakekua Bay, Hawaii
(FIGURE 46) DOLPHIN. SPACE TRAVELER, INC.

After a moment, I realized this might be my only chance. Reef sharks aren't that dangerous, I rationalized, and what about all those stories I'd heard where dolphins protected humans from sharks? I decided I wasn't going to let fear get in the way of my dream. I took several deep breaths, replaced fear with desire and jumped back into the water.

Fortunately, I didn't see the shark again and within moments the spinner dolphins were circling all around me. They glided within reach and we swam eye to eye. I was a stranger in their world, but they accepted me and I accepted them.

By breathing deeply and remaining calm, I fulfilled my childhood dream. It was one of the more magical moments I've had the pleasure of experiencing on this planet.

ACT II

DEPARTING

A ship in harbor is safe—
but that is not what ships are built for.

———

JOHN A. SHEDD, writer (1859 – ?)

Earthview from the Space Shuttle

(Figure 47) Earthview Flare. NASA

CHAPTER THREE

Experiencing Earthview

One's destination is never a place but rather a new way of looking at things.

———

HENRY MILLER, writer (1891 – 1980)

Author's Log
JULY 4, 2099, 7:35 A.M.—BON VOYAGE

The time has come to depart and experience earthview. After a short, thrilling ride to orbit, we are moments away from viewing our everyday lives from a much larger perspective—250 miles above our home planet.

Our departure date, July 4, 2099, is a symbolic day of emancipation for all human-kind. On this day, six everyday people will embark on the first adventure vacation to Mars and join the search for other life in the universe.

From a launch-strategy perspective, July 4, 2099, is a fortuitous time when the differing orbits of Earth and Mars bring the two worlds very close together—only 96 million miles. At its farthest point, Mars is about 640 million miles away from Earth. The distance we'll travel by leaving today, at this point of conjunction, is much shorter and will cut months off our travel time.

If all goes well, we'll be spending New Year's Day on the Red Planet. Sure, we'll miss being with our loved ones, but the sacrifice we're making will benefit everyone back home.

For the time being, while we're in orbit around Earth, we'll experience not only weightlessness but also a mind-altering view of our home planet. As with those who have gone before us, experiencing earthview can change the rest of our lives.

Then we're on to Mars, mystery and hopefully a safe return home.

Seeing Earth from a distance can profoundly affect a person's perceptions about themselves and the world they live in every day. Japanese science fiction calls this change of consciousness "new evolution." Author Frank White called it the "overview effect" in his book by the same name.[1]

The night the Apollo 8 astronauts first circled the Moon, television newscaster Walter Cronkite said: "I think that picture of the earthrise over the Moon's horizon, that blue disk out there in space, floating alone in the darkness, the utter black of space, had the effect of impressing on all of us our loneliness out here. The fact that we seem to be the only spot where anything like humans could be living. And the major impression I think it made on most of us was how ridiculous it is that we have this difficulty getting along on this little lifeboat of ours, floating out there in space. And the necessity of our understanding each other and of the brotherhood of humankind on this floating island of ours, made a great impression, I think, on everybody."

Like those space travelers who have already seen Earth from space, we too will return home from Expedition LifePoint with new and profound perceptions about ourselves and how we live every day on this planet of ours.

GETTING TO SPACE

In order to experience earthview, we first have to get to orbit by climbing to the top of what's called the gravity well. So, physically speaking, the question is, "How do we get our butts into space?"

Escaping Earth's gravity is as much about speed as it is about altitude. Reaching orbit is a matter of moving fast enough to fall off the edge of the earth.

Think of it this way: Because Earth is round, when we stand in the middle of a desert or prairie and look at the horizon, we are essentially looking downhill. That's because the curvature of Earth is approximately 8.7 inches per mile. For a six-foot-tall person, the ground at the horizon is roughly three miles away and two feet lower than the ground on which he stands.

Leaving the cradle. The Apollo 8 crew took this image of Earth as they rounded the Moon for the first time.

(FIGURE 50) EARTHRISE. NASA

If we could propel ourselves like Superman and move horizontally five miles every second, we would always stay the same distance above Earth's curved surface and achieve a very low orbit a few feet above the ground. Achieving a higher orbit of 200 miles above Earth means accelerating us, in our spacecraft, to a speed of 17,500 miles per hour!

Everyday Travel Tip
GET A NEW VIEW AND GET A NEW YOU

You can have an earthview experience in many ways without going into space. Next time you find yourself flying in an airplane above the countryside, standing at the top of a hill or even atop a tall building, watch the future of two separate cars traveling on two separate roads. From your heightened point of view, you can see that the two drivers will eventually meet up, although they do not yet know it. Different people can perceive the same reality in different ways depending on their physical location.

If you find yourself needing a new perspective, get up from your chair, look out the window or take a short walk outside. Getting a new view can change the way you feel and think about something.

LET'S GO!

It's eight in the morning. The air is still, but we are excited with the impending thrill of finally traveling to space.

We stand together on the tarmac of the first private spaceport in California's Mojave Desert. It looks like any other mid-sized airport except for the large crowd of excited people. Camera crews gather near an inconspicuous hangar bearing the banner "Expedition LifePoint." A red-tail hawk dives in for a closer look.

A cheer goes up as the hangar doors slide open and a spectacular vehicle rolls into the center of attention. Photographers' flash bulbs accent the hot July sun glistening off the white composite skin of a captivating spacecraft bearing the name *JourneyStar*.

JourneyStar is the shuttlecraft that will rocket us to orbit for our rendezvous with *CosmicSea*, the state-of-the-art spaceyacht that will carry us to Mars.

Here's what is about to happen. First, *JourneyStar* will ride the underbelly of a large spacecraft carrier to an altitude of 48,000 feet, just like the historic flight of *SpaceShipOne*, the world's first private sub-orbital spacecraft. At this altitude, *JourneyStar* will separate from her mothership. In the blink of an eye, her rocket engines will ignite and thrust us the rest of the way into orbit 250 miles above our heads.

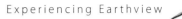

LAUNCH TIME

The pilot welcomes us aboard as we each take our seat. His voice over the intercom reminds us:

"Please fasten your seat belts. We don't want anyone floating into the aisles when we reach zero-gravity."

After a takeoff as smooth and comfortable as any passenger jet, we soon reach the desired altitude for separation.

We hear the countdown.

"10, 9, 8, 7, 6, 5, 4, 3, 2, 1. Go for separation. Ignite!"

With a thunderous roar, *JourneyStar* begins to vibrate fiercely.

Godspeed John Doe! There's no turning back now.

We sink deeper into our seats as *JourneyStar* hurtles into space. The surrounding landscape outside the ship's windows blurs into a sky-toned streak of color.

"Boom!" We cross the sound barrier speeding toward Mach 2.

Our hearts race along with our spacecraft. We soon become keenly aware of the obvious risks of traveling at such an incredible speed.

In just two minutes the first-stage rocket burns out. Now we're going Mach 12 and pulling about 3 Gs, like on a roller coaster ride and only three times the acceleration you experience on a swing. Still, it's a hell of a ride!

After traveling over 300 nautical miles downrange, the second-stage rocket takes over and pushes us through the atmosphere at ever-increasing speeds. Our ride begins to smooth as we rise through the thinning atmosphere.

In another few minutes, we separate from the second-stage rocket and penetrate the planet's atmospheric membrane as we climb into the majestic realm of outer space. Finally, we reach our orbital speed of 25,568 feet per second, or 17,432 mph, at an altitude of 100 nautical miles.

SpaceShipOne separates from the *White Knight*.
(FIGURE 51) *SpaceShipOne* Separates. Scaled Composites/Mike Masse

JOURNEYSTAR'S TRAJECTORY

Below us, we can see the Gulf of Mexico.

After passing over Florida, we head out above the Atlantic Ocean in a southeast direction, our first low Earth orbit.

In about half an hour, South Africa appears. We cross over the city of Durban and reach the southernmost latitude of our flight, above the Indian Ocean. Then we head northward, skirt the northern coast of Australia and fly over the broad Pacific Ocean.

Only 88 minutes after takeoff, we find ourselves back over the midwestern United States. We begin our second orbit 22 degrees westward of our first.

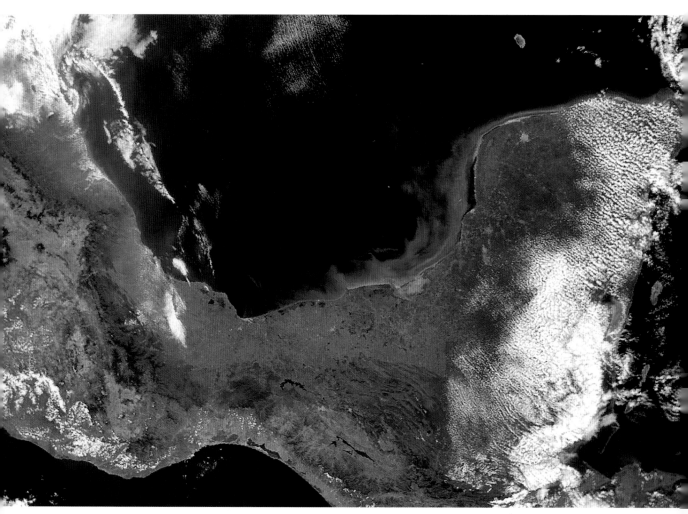

Gulf of Mexico, Yucatán Peninsula

(FIGURE 52) GULF OF MEXICO. THE SEAWIFS PROJECT, NASA/GODDARD SPACE FLIGHT CENTER AND ORBIMAGE

Sunrise through a porthole of the International Space Station

(Figure 53) Sunrise. NASA

From Space I saw Earth,
indescribably beautiful
with the scars of
national boundaries gone.

———

Mohammed Ahmad Faris, Syrian astronaut
(1951 –)

In only one Earth day, we pass over most of the planet's surface between 33 degrees of north and south latitude, roughly between San Diego and Buenos Aires. We experience 16 glorious sunrises. The Sun appears and disappears every 45 minutes. We begin to adjust our lives accordingly.

FIRST LOOK

The view of Earth out the window is probably the most dramatic aspect of space travel. Astronauts say the emotional effect of the view is even greater than the experience of weightlessness.

On Earth, space is something we see above our heads at night. From our spacecraft, we are in the scene and not merely watching it anymore. The reality of space traveling can be overwhelming. Earth out the window is never removed from immediate consciousness.

Gemini 4 astronaut Ed White enjoyed the first view of Earth from outside of a spacecraft during his historic 23-minute long spacewalk on June 3, 1965. He later said the spacewalk was the most comfortable part of the mission.

(FIGURE 54) FIRST SPACEWALK. NASA

When we walk or drive across Earth's surface, we are like a fly walking on the ceiling of the Sistine Chapel. It's difficult to appreciate the beauty of da Vinci's artwork from such close proximity. We have to pull back to appreciate the masterpiece. As space travelers, we need to back off a hundred or more miles to see the masterpiece that is our home planet.

Earth is one of the most entertaining and enlightening objects we can ponder from orbit. Even though all of *CosmicSea*'s monitors can display movies and delayed television feeds from home, the best entertainment in orbit is often out the window. Instead of watching hours of television, space travelers look out the windows at Earth and wonder: *What are my family and friends doing down there right now? Why are countries still fighting after all these centuries of war and bloodshed? Where are the boundaries that divide mankind?* No boundaries between countries can be seen from space.

On Earth, we wage wars over "your god versus my god versus their god." In space, it's easy to envision how all of our "gods" may be simply different interpretations of the universe. The astute traveler viewing Earth while floating in orbit is akin to the absolute protector of earth, ocean and sky.

If you want to build a ship, don't drum up people together to collect wood and don't assign them tasks and work, but rather teach them to long for the endless immensity of the sea.

———

ANTOINE DE SAINT-EXUPÉRY, French pilot/poet (1900 – 1944)

Hungarian stamp commemorating the French pilot and author of *The Little Prince*, Antoine de Saint-Exupéry

(FIGURE 55) SAINT-EXUPÉRY. CLETE DELVAUX

Third Insight
EXPERIENCING EARTHVIEW

Think differently. Change your view and change your perspective on life.

When we were primal creatures roaming the plains for survival, we would climb a tree to get a better understanding of our surroundings. We saw the lay of the land and then we would move on to experience another new place and perspective.

In the same way, travel is an opportunity for personal growth and greater understanding. Traveling reminds us to view things from different points of view.

Reframe the way you look at your career, your life, your loves. Look at everyday situations from a different vantage point. Get a view from above and change the world below.

The real voyage of discovery consists not in seeing new landscapes, but in having new eyes.

———

MARCEL PROUST,
French writer (1871 – 1922)

THE QUEST OF EXPEDITION LIFEPOINT

Skylab astronaut Ed Gibson believes the more people who experience space, the greater difference it will make.[2] Why not use the power of television to help more people vicariously experience space?

When man first set foot on the Moon, the entire world watched. It was the largest television viewing audience of all time. Most people who saw it were changed forever.

Expedition LifePoint could create a similar leap in awareness for all of humankind. You and your fellow travelers on Expedition Life-Point could be the ones to vicariously pass a new perspective on to everyone watching on Earth.

A media expedition such as LifePoint could carry both specialists and qualified everyday volunteers into orbit and on to Mars. Expedition LifePoint could be privately funded from corporate donations, sponsorships and perhaps a wealthy paying guest or two. Non-profit organizations such as EarthWatch Institute have been using similar

There's no place like home.

(FIGURE 56) EARTH POOL BALL. NASA

methods to fund scientific expeditions on planet Earth for years. As a matter of fact, England's Royal Geographic Society describes a media expedition as an adventure that creates material for a book, a magazine article, a film or a television show.

Commercially driven reality television shows have proven themselves to be a media-savvy environment for corporate sponsors. Operating Expedition LifePoint as an unprecedented media event could make it a very viable journey.

Author's Log
SIX HOURS AFTER LAUNCH—ORBITING EARTH

Finally, we arrive at *CosmicSea,* orbiting 300 miles above Earth. Since reaching orbit, we've been circling our home planet every 90 minutes! Soon, we will depart for Mars on Expedition LifePoint.

JourneyStar maneuvers into docking position as a human-like robonaut floats by, looks at us and waves. Over the ship's intercom, we hear a sweet female voice.

"Ahoy, there. Welcome to the *CosmicSea."*

We hear a few thruster blasts and see several bursts of vapor vent from the Orbital Docking System (ODS).

"Kachunk." The ODS clamps lock on and gently pull *JourneyStar* snugly against the mothership where we will spend the next several months of our lives.

This is going to be one long trip. It's time to lighten up, enjoy the ride and experience the next insight.

We approach our mothership, *CosmicSea*, after the exhilarating ride to orbit safely inside our shuttlecraft, *JourneyStar*.

(Figure 57) *JourneyStar* Arrives. Space Traveler, Inc.

Astrobatics on Skylab

(Figure 61) Skylab Astrobats. NASA

Astronaut Mark Lee flying free over the seas and clouds of Earth on STS-64 in 1994

(Figure 62) Free-falling. NASA/JSC

TO FLY IN FREEDOM

Defying gravity gives us unlimited movement in all directions. Floating weightless frees us from many physical restrictions. This newfound freedom for our bodies can inspire a powerful state of mind.

A few years ago I helped make an underwater film for the Handicapped Scuba Association. Many of these people were unable to walk like you and I. They are paraplegics or amputees. One young man was blind. While filming these physically challenged and amazing people, I realized in a very dramatic way just how gravity limits us all.

A space traveler flies in the freedom of weightlessness using a Manned Maneuvering Unit.

(Figure 63) MMU Close-up. NASA

On this special sunny morning in a small cove south of Laguna Beach, California, I helped these inspiring scuba divers unload their heavy gear and put on wetsuits. Then I watched in awe as they crawled 50 yards across the beach on their elbows, dragging their limp limbs behind them. At ocean's edge, they strapped on scuba tanks and entered the great Pacific Ocean. After battling pounding surf, they finally swam off with newfound freedom into the weightless water world of a giant kelp forest.

There was one particular diver, appropriately named Will, whom I'll always remember. Will had an incredibly strong character despite his frail physique. We had to push Will in his wheelchair to the ocean floor 40 feet beneath the surface. There he sat, seemingly helpless in his wheelchair, with the kelp swaying above his head. Then with the greatest of ease, Will floated up and out of that wheelchair as if he had just reached zero-gravity. Will was flying in three dimensions, free of gravity and free of his own limitations.

Will made me realize that handicapped scuba divers and eager space travelers like you and me are not all that different. We all strive to break the physical bounds of gravity and go beyond our limitations—to fly in freedom. This is the heart of the space-traveler experience.

A physically challenged scuba diver floats out of his wheelchair and experiences the newfound freedom of weightlessness.

(Figure 64) HSA Diver. Handicapped Scuba Association

Everyday Travel Tip
EXPERIENCE WEIGHTLESSNESS

Every now and then, go to your local playground and swing on a swing. Delight in the weightless moment at the height of each swing just before gravity pulls you back to Earth. Experience the thrill of floating between up and down.

Domes have been around for centuries. But a geodesic dome like this one, built next to the Queen Mary cruise ship in Long Beach, California, encloses the most volume with the least surface material through which to lose heat or intercept potentially damaging winds.

(FIGURE 65) GEODOME. SPACE TRAVELER, INC.

THE SHAPES OF SPACE

One of the most common shapes in the weightlessness of space is a round sphere. Planets, moons and stars are round, a natural shape in space. When an astronaut squirts a drop of water in zero-gravity, the water droplet forms a sphere.

Geodesic-dome designer Buckminster Fuller pointed out that "a sphere is a mathematically finite, omni-symmetrical, closed system."[2] A sphere represents the intrinsic nature of infinity and the circle of life.

Another predominant shape in the universe is the triangle. A triangle is composed of three straight lines, the smallest number of straight lines that can connect end to end and create a rigid structure. Triangles are found in everything from the shape made by our two legs standing on the ground to ancient pyramids and modern geodesic domes.

Microscopic geodesic spheres, also known as fullerenes or Buckyballs, were found in the 4.6-billion-year-old Allende meteorite that landed at 1:05 a.m. on February 8, 1969, in Pueblito de Allende, Chihuahua, Mexico. Estimated to weigh several tons, the Allende created a huge fireball, then shattered and rained fragments over a 60-square-mile area. The Allende meteorite is carbonaceous chondrite, considered the most primitive form of matter in the universe. Scientists theorize that if, at the beginning of time, the universe cooled and the dust clumped together and formed a rock, then the result would be something like the Allende meteorite.

(FIGURE 66) ALLENDE METEORITE. D. BALL, ASU

First drawing of *CosmicSea* on a napkin. Since spheres create volume and triangles create rigid structures, then geodesic spheres connected to long cylindrical trusses encased in inflatable modules can form a sturdy tetrahedral structure, perfect for the weightlessness of space. (FIGURE 67) *COSMICSEA* NAPKIN. SPACE TRAVELER, INC.

THE WEIGHTLESS DESIGN OF *COSMICSEA*

Since spheres and triangles are fundamental shapes of the universe, then spheres and triangles may be the best shapes for spaceships.

One night, while doodling on a napkin waiting for dinner at a nearby restaurant, I envisioned a spacecraft designed with the two basic shapes of the universe—spheres and triangles. By the time my meal arrived, I had sketched a pyramid-shaped spacecraft with spheres at the corners—the basic structure of *CosmicSea*.

I was inspired by a conversation about spacecraft that I'd had earlier that day with noted space architect and good friend John Spencer and the head of NASA's commercial space division. John and I listened intently as this gentleman told us how the overall design of the International Space Station ("ISS") could have been improved by reducing the flexing action, or lack of rigidity, between the station's linked modules, particularly during the docking and undocking of the Space Shuttle.

So, I thought, if the simplest geometric structure that has rigidity within itself is a triangle, then a pyramid-shaped spacecraft like *CosmicSea* would be the strongest structure possible in the weightlessness of space. As I came to discover, such tetrahedral space facilities were being designed by NASA architect Marc Cohen as far back as the 1970s.

This rear view of *CosmicSea* shows the vehicle before installation of the aft deck that carries *LifeLander,* the landing craft that will carry us safely down to the surface of Mars. (FIGURE 68) *COSMICSEA* REAR. SPACE TRAVELER, INC.

MEETING OUR FIRST MATE—ANIMA

CosmicSea's computer system is programmed with a human personality interface or avatar that goes by the name Animasphere or, as she likes to be called, Anima. Anima gets her name from her function—Artificial and Natural Intelligence Matrix Assistant. Anima is the digital personification of all the ship's sensors, gauges, life-support and computer systems. She helps us control everything from room temperature and fuel consumption to communication and navigation. Even the tiny nanosensors we swallowed before launch are linked directly into Anima's computer and help monitor each of our health and well-being.

Although Anima can appear on any monitor throughout the ship, most of the time she prefers to float beside each of us, one-on-one, appearing on our Personal Satellite Spheres (PSS). Digitally speaking, she is an attractive, intelligent woman with a wry sense of humor. The sound of her voice is warm and comforting. The more we get to know her, the more Anima seems to become a real person, a close friend, a trusted companion.

Astronaut John L. Phillips floats in the Destiny laboratory of the International Space Station with a superimposed image of Anima, a Personal Satellite Sphere.

(Figure 69) Animasphere-ISS. NASA and Space Traveler, Inc.

Anima enjoys talking with the guests and will take any opportunity to crack a joke.

"There's one thing that orbit teaches all of us about positive thinking: never let anything get you down, not even gravity."

Anima is more than computer intelligence; she is the masthead of our ship. Symbolically, Anima's image functions like the Greek goddess Athena's image that was carved onto the prow of the ship *Argo* in the ancient myth of Jason and the Argonauts. Now, however, myth has become math and the spirit has become silicon—yet our figurehead's significance remains to guide and protect. The Latin root of the word *anima* means "life."

WOMEN IN SPACE

As warm, soft light reflects from the massive solar sail outside the nearby viewport, Anima, our female computer avatar, turns up her own volume as if speaking for all womankind. The image of Anima on our monitor screens fades to historical newscast footage as she speaks.

"On June 16, 1963, Russian cosmonaut Valentina Tereshkova blasted into orbit to carry out one of the most important campaigns of the Soviet Cold War effort. She was the first female in space. Then, almost 20 years later, in 1982, Russia's Svetlana Savitskaya became the first woman to 'walk' in space. And with very little respect, I might add. The commander of the Salyut space station supposedly greeted Savitskaya with flowers, an offer of an apron and an invitation to do the cooking. The following year, astronaut Sally Ride became the first American woman in space."

Animasphere floats between us and continues:

"Manly strength needed on Earth for such things as lifting becomes less important in space because of the absence of gravity. There's also growing evidence that women are better able to cope with the isolation of space travel. Astronaut Shannon Lucid, who spent 223 days in orbit aboard the Russian *Mir* space station, reportedly had a much easier time adjusting to the isolation of long-term space flight than did many of her male counterparts. Crews of men and women seem to work better than one-gender crews during long periods in spacecraft, keeping the atmosphere lighter and more balanced."

Valentina Tereshkova, the first woman in space
(FIGURE 70) VALENTINA TERESHKOVA. ASSOCIATED PRESS

Dr. Sally Ride was the first American woman in space. She rode the Space Shuttle *Challenger* to orbit on STS-7, June 18, 1983.
(FIGURE 71) SALLY RIDE. NASA

Christa McAuliffe experiences weightlessness during a KC-135 training flight. Christa was selected as the primary candidate for NASA's Teacher in Space Project on July 19, 1985. Tragically, Christa and the other crewmembers of STS-51-L died on January 28, 1986, when the Space Shuttle *Challenger* exploded moments after launch.
(FIGURE 72) CHRISTA McAULIFFE. NASA

"Co-ed space travelers on extended flights must work as a team and not show favoritism to their lovers. If a personal relationship goes sour early in a mission, there is no place to escape from an ex-lover and a substitute partner could be very difficult to find. Affairs could undermine preexisting marriages back on Earth. As you'll discover on the next leg of your journey, how you interact with your fellow space travelers is a crucial factor in your survival."

Anima finishes her impassioned speech and floats over to a porthole, where she looks longingly out into space without saying another word. Anima is so "almost human" that it seems she yearns for a human body.

COSMIC SUTRA

As futurist Arthur C. Clarke once speculated regarding human travels in space, "Weightlessness will bring new forms of erotica. About time, too."

Surely, space travelers, especially those on their honeymoon, will be inspired to make love in microgravity.

Sex in space has remained a relatively unexplored area— or should we say undocumented? As for who had the first sex in space, all we know is that Mark C. Lee and N. Jan Davis were the first married couple in space in 1992. Some experts believe the co-ed cosmonauts on *Mir* may claim title to "first sex in space" as well.

Astronaut Shannon Lucid floats through the Russian *Mir* space station Spektr module. A veteran of five space shuttle flights and six months on the *Mir*, Shannon is the first to admit that the novelty of space travel quickly wears off. (FIGURE 73) SHANNON LUCID. NASA

Zero-gravity romance

(Figure 74) Cosmic Sutra. Space
Traveler, Inc.

Whoever was first, one thing is for sure: the act of making love in
weightlessness is a challenge in itself.

Spaceflight affects the sheer mechanics of having sex. On one
hand, you can get as creative with positions as weightlessness allows.
On the other hand, you may have to learn a new technique or
use a specially designed harness to avoid floating away from your
partner.

Another challenge of having sex in space was brought to my
attention one night at the Comedy Store in Hollywood as legendary
comedian Robin Williams performed improvisations based upon
audience suggestions. When I shouted out "sex in space," Robin pro-
ceeded to weightlessly dart about the stage yelling, "Watch out for
the wet spot!"

Seriously, though, imagine floating together with your lover,
in the privacy of your honeymoon suite. The powerful feelings of
sensuality and weightlessness stimulate your body, mind and soul
to new, heightened levels of pleasure and consciousness. Outside the
window, you catch glimpses of a familiar blue-white orb—Earth—
floating in the cosmos. What a heavenly place to conceive a new life
and perhaps even give birth.

Sex in space may be a little trickier, but weightlessness will not
subdue our basic primal urge to procreate; lovemaking is a matter of
survival.

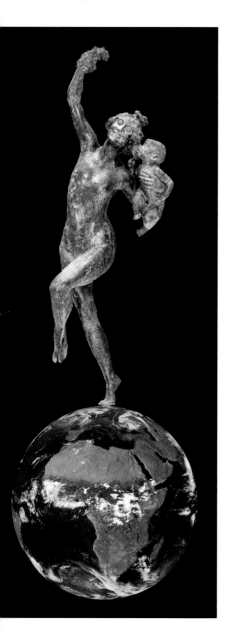

Even though this statue of "Bacchante and Infant Faun" by Frederick MacMonnies is made of metal, the artwork is permeated with the quality of lightness. (FIGURE 75) BACCHANTE. COPYRIGHT © 2005 DANIEL P. B. SMITH AND RELEASED UNDER THE TERMS OF THE GFDL

Unless we are content with test-tube babies, having sex in space will be necessary to replenish pioneering families on multi-generational missions to planets around other suns. Children born in space and who stay in space for long periods of time, however, will need to counteract the bone loss caused by weightlessness so that they may one day stand on Earth for the first time.

Weightlessness may also enhance the end of life. As more of us live to be 100 years old or greater, the side effects of aging such as back pain, arthritis and heart disease may be eased in the zero-gravity environment. Instead of shrinking when we get older, we could elongate up to three inches because there is less gravity compressing our vertebrae.

Reality check: When the thrill is gone.

Although astronauts often speak of the beauty, awe and transcendence of the space experience, seasoned astronaut Shannon Lucid reminds us that even the uniqueness of weightlessness can become routine.

"Experiencing weightlessness and seeing Earth from space won't be enough to entertain people," she says. "The novelty wears off quickly and space travelers of all sorts need something to keep themselves occupied."[3]

LIGHTNESS AND EASE

The fundamental force of gravity that holds us on Earth, like the natural force of electromagnetism we use in our household appliances, is very much a part of our everyday lives. The only way to escape the grasp of gravity is with the phenomenon of weightlessness. We can use the powerful essence of weightlessness in our everyday lives by adopting a mental attitude of "lightness and ease." Lightness and ease are feelings that can help take the "weight" of everyday life off our shoulders.

In his landmark book, *To the Actor,* Michael Chekhov, cousin to famed playwright Anton Chekhov, explains lightness and ease as a quality that can be expressed in great pieces of art. If we look at such massive art objects as Rodin's The Thinker, Michelangelo's Moses, or any other artistic creation of this standard, we will see that the weight of the material is overcome; the object is permeated with a sense of lightness. Great art leaves us feeling uplifted.[4]

Like artists, we all can benefit from the ability to express ourselves in a light and easy way. I learned the concept of lightness and ease from legendary acting coach George Shdanoff, who worked closely for many years in Russia with Michael Chekhov. Shdanoff taught the concept of lightness and ease to such great American actors as Paul Newman and Gregory Peck. We can enhance our daily lives by adopting an attitude of lightness and ease.

Astronaut Story Musgrave enjoys a moment of weightlessness as he runs. With every step each of us takes, there is a moment of free-falling, or weightlessness. Enjoy it. Lighten up.
(FIGURE 76) STORY MUSGRAVE. STORY MUSGRAVE

Everyday Travel Tip
FEELING LIGHTNESS AND EASE

To experience the essence of lightness and ease, try this simple exercise.

Stand still with your feet on the floor. Bend your knees slightly and square your shoulders. Take a moment and realize that you must stand strong against the invisible force of gravity. This first attitude can be expressed as: "I am bound to the earth, and the force of gravity draws my weight down to it."

Now, recognize there is another attitude that you can express while standing on Earth. Straighten your knees. Let your arms "float" above your head as you come up on your toes and reach for the stars. Think to yourself, "My upright position frees me from the earth on which I stand. My inner inclination is upward and not downward." Concentrate for a while on this liberating feeling of lightness and ease.

You can perform this simple exercise whenever you need a lift. Having an attitude of weightlessness, lightness and ease can help you throughout the day.

Fourth Insight
FEELING WEIGHTLESS

The essence of the fourth insight is: lighten up.

Even though astronauts' senses tell them they are floating weightless, they are actually free-falling around the earth. Floating weightless and free-falling are one and the same, depending on how you look at it.

Walking on the surface of Earth is nothing more than the process of falling forward and catching yourself, step by step. There is a moment of weightlessness in between every step we take every day.

Enjoy your moments of weightlessness on Earth. Lighten your step and live each day with as much ease as possible.

An Expedition LifePoint crewmember and Animasphere pose for this picture by a CabinHab porthole, as a Mars supply ship precedes our journey. It is carrying the food and other essentials we will need to survive once we land on the Red Planet.
(FIGURE 77) CABINHAB VIEW. SPACE TRAVELER, INC.

Author's Log
END OF DAY ONE

After a long first day in space, we finally float into the CabinHab module and settle into our cozy individual cabins, as comfortable as those found on fine ocean-going yachts. A large picture window frames the awesome view of Earth as an unmanned supply ship passes by, preceding us to our destination—Mars.

Each of our cabins looks something like a normal bedroom—but with a startling difference. There is no bed. Instead, we'll soon snuggle into a fire-resistant sleeping bag attached to a wall. Apollo 17 astronaut Jack Schmitt used to say that sleeping in a zero-gravity environment is far more refreshing than sleeping on Earth, even with the many unaccustomed noises in the craft and the constant drone of the air-conditioning and life-support systems.[5]

Our first day has been long, exhilarating but exhausting. Everyone is already fast asleep, their arms floating comfortably in front of them. I wonder, are they dreaming about the life they left behind back home—or the discoveries that lie ahead on Mars and the potential for a new era in human evolution?

Besides me, only Anima, the floating robo-sphere, is awake and active. She is making her rounds throughout the ship and giving digital commands comparable to a seaman's "batten down the hatches" and "reef the main" for our trip into geosynchronous orbit.

Anima notices that I'm still awake, floats quietly into my cabin and talks me through a few zero-gravity yoga poses that help me relax.

"Breathe in and out," she says, making a breathy noise as if she had lungs. Anima is such a convincing computer personality that when I close my eyes I can envision my wife taking a deep sensual breath while arching her weightless body, backlit by the crescent moon shining outside my porthole.

I used to joke that there's no better remedy for a heavy heart than weightlessness, but even zero-gravity doesn't diminish the weight of wanting to be with someone you love and had to leave behind.

As I doze off I hear, "Good night and sweet dreams, space traveler."

CosmicSea in geosynchronous orbit

(Figure 78) *CosmicSea* Orbits. Space Traveler, Inc.

CHAPTER FIVE

Interacting with the Biosphere

Author's Log
DAY THREE IN ORBIT
JULY 7, 2099—OUR SHIP IS OUR WORLD

After several days of travel, we are now orbiting 23,000 miles directly above the same spot on Earth, an orbit known as geosynchronous orbit. There is something comforting about traveling with a view of home right outside our window.

Tomorrow we leave the safe embrace of our orbit around Earth and travel through black, boundless interplanetary space to Mars. After one more 24-hour geosynchronous loop, we'll initiate the engine burn that will propel us on to the mysterious Red Planet. Uncertain about the unknown, we're still willing to go beyond this point of no return. We'll never have this chance again.

For the next six months, this craft will be our entire means of life support. *CosmicSea* will be our only world, a miniature spaceship Earth. Our loved ones back home are protected by Earth's fragile atmosphere, warmed by the sun and cooled by the breeze. We, on the other hand, are only protected by the integrity of our ship and its critical life-support systems. The same biospheric principles that keep our families alive back on Earth will keep us alive during the journey to our destination, the first human colony on Mars—New Shangri-la.

This we know.
All things are connected
like the blood
which unites one family…

Whatever befalls the Earth
befalls the sons and
daughters of the Earth.
Man did not weave
the web of life
He is merely a strand in it.
Whatever he does to the web,
he does to himself.

———

TED PERRY, contemporary screenwriter
Inspired by Chief Seattle, Suquamish
Native American (1784 – 1866)

Our relationship with Earth is best symbolized in the ship's Exosphere, the largest sphere on *CosmicSea*. Here, inside this spacious inflatable module, we grow supplemental fresh food, produce extra oxygen and recycle much of our water supply.

Completely cut off from Earth, we will only survive if we keep the environment of our spacecraft in balance. If we can't manage our on-board provisions and the ship's ecosystem, we face certain disaster. How we interact with each other will play a crucial role in everyone's survival. Can we all get along?

IT'S ALIVE!

IN THE EARLY DAYS OF THE NASA SPACE PROGRAM, atmospheric chemist James Lovelock had an illuminating insight: the planet Earth is a living, self-organizing system.

Lovelock's insight came in a flash of enlightenment in a small room on the top floor of a building at the Jet Propulsion Laboratory in 1965.

"An awesome thought came to me. The earth's atmosphere was an extraordinary and unstable mixture of gases, yet I knew that it was constant in composition over quite long periods of time. Could it be that life on Earth not only made the atmosphere, but also regulated it—keeping it at a constant composition, and at a level favorable for organisms?"[1]

The Gaia Theory, as Lovelock's insight came to be known, presented a radical break with conventional science even though the view of Earth as being an integrated living entity has a long tradition. The Earth Goddess, Gaia, was revered as the supreme deity in early pre-Hellenic Greece. Even before the Book of Genesis was written, ancient cultures around the world considered Earth to be not only living but to have a nervous system related to its magnetic field. Hundreds of years later, in the 18th century, Goethe took the romantic view of Earth when he wrote, "Each creature is but a patterned gradation of one great harmonious whole."[2]

Although the idea of Earth being alive is ancient, the space flights of the 1960s gave modern humans the first look at our planet from outer space and a chance to truly perceive it as an integrated whole. The first photographs of Earth by early astronauts continue to be powerful reminders of our fragile relationship to the environment.

The biosphere of Earth is made up of everything—from deep inside its hidden molten core, to you and me, and all life maintained by its thin and fragile atmosphere. (**FIGURE 79**) BLUEBIO. NASA

THE WEB OF LIFE

Today, people who study Earth as a living system refer to our planet as Biosphere 1 because Earth is the largest self-contained, regenerating ecosystem we know of. The field of biospherics draws upon everything from biology, geology and climatology to politics, planetary management and big business. To put it simply, the grand biosphere of Earth is comprised of the rocks, trees, water, wind, animals, you and me—all interwoven into an incredible web of life.

Every day as we go about our lives, we rely on Earth's resources and each other for fresh bread, medical assistance, a ride to work or a loan for a home. We are in constant interplay with friends, family, acquaintances, computers, the food we eat, the air we breathe and the trash we create. The exhaust from the cars we drive contributes to global warming and raises the temperature of the oceans. The same limited supply of water in Earth's oceans and lakes evaporates to become rain for our crops and the water we drink.

Everything is connected. Our survival depends on maintaining this delicate balance. All it takes is one careless person who pollutes a community's water system for the entire community to get sick. Similarly, one person fouling the water system in *CosmicSea* could leave the rest of us literally dying of thirst.

Space engineers are continually improving the designs of sustainable life-support systems using the basic principles of Earth's ecosystems. The best example of such a closed system is the EcoSphere®—a self-sustaining miniature world encased in glass. Sealed off from everything but light, algae inside the sphere create oxygen for the shrimp. In turn, the shrimp give off carbon dioxide that algae need to survive. Ecospheres are based on NASA research and are proof that life can exist in a sealed environment if properly balanced. EcoSpheres may be ordered directly from Ecosphere Associates, Inc., by calling their toll-free order line at 800-729-9870 or by emailing customer_service@eco-sphere.com.

(FIGURE 80) ECOSPHERE. ECOSPHERE ASSOCIATES, INC.

LIFE IN THE EXOSPHERE

Since we will spend the next several months inside *CosmicSea*'s artificial biosphere—a microcosm of Earth—we must interact with our ship's environment in a balanced way. If we can mimic the flows of energy, water, food and waste that occur on Earth, then we stand a very good chance of surviving our journey.

Earth is the largest self-contained life-supporting system we know of in the universe. Therefore, traveling through space requires the design of spacecraft that mimic Earth's system. NASA calls such designs Closed Ecological Life Support Systems, or CELSS. Imagine small greenhouses that grow your food and oversized aquariums that produce fresh fish and filter wastewater.

Take for example the used murky water from the ship's drains and toilets that progressively clears as it passes through special filters and the roots of plants. The plants absorb the nutrients from this wastewater, producing oxygen and purifying the recycled water we drink.

Scientists inside NASA's Biomass Production Chamber at Kennedy Space Center are learning to grow crops in closed environments similar to what might be used in space travel. (Figure 81) CELSS. NASA

If we want a drink of water in the Exosphere and don't have an appropriate container, we can locate a spigot marked drinkable and simply plop out a spheroid of H_2O. The weightless water ball will float in space until we suck it into our mouth.

As for another necessary life-support system—the restroom—thigh clamps and handgrips help keep our butts firmly positioned on the NASA-designed toilet seat in weightlessness. When we're done, a powerful ventilator sucks away all the solid and liquid waste, where it is dried, disinfected and recycled.

And bathing, well—due to the danger of showers leaking water and shorting out the ship's electrical system—sponge baths are the norm in space. Excess water is sucked down a vacuum tube.

Some visions of space colonies suggest that people could live along with their plants and animals in a single large enclosure resembling a village on Earth. A NASA Ames/Stanford University Summer Study worked out the broad engineering requirements for the toroidal-shaped space colony design depicted here. The challenge of sustaining a closed ecosystem was the basis for the painting. This design became known as the "Stanford Torus" and was painted by space artist Don Davis for NASA. Unfortunately, it will be many years before space biospheres resemble in any way a natural Earth habitat.

(Figure 82) Stanford Torus. Don Davis for NASA

Interior of *CosmicSea*'s Exosphere—a place to recreate, grow plants, recycle water and balance the life-support systems that sustain our lives. (FIGURE 83) EXOSPHERE INSIDE. SPACE TRAVELER, INC.

AT HOME IN THE EXOSPHERE

The shimmering Exosphere, the largest module of *CosmicSea*, is our transportable substitute for the biosphere of Earth and requires the same kind of care. Fully deployed, this geodesic inflatable sphere will not only supplement our food and oxygen supply but will also provide us with additional space for recreation and exercise.

The Exosphere is named in part after the protective outermost edge of Earth's atmosphere. But the word "exosphere" also refers to the exoskeleton of *CosmicSea*'s largest structure. The geodesic cable ribbing in Exosphere's external fabric increases the tensile strength of the overall surface structure. Because the exoskeleton is flexible, the sphere is deployable like a ship's sail, a Japanese paper lantern or Buckminster Fuller's Dymaxion House. The Exosphere is a large enclosed ecosystem perfect for zero-gravity life.

(FIGURE 84) QUINOA PLANT.
ANONYMOUS

(FIGURE 85) QUINOA PILAF.
SPACE TRAVELER, INC.

BALANCING THE SHIP'S BIOSPHERE

For a taste of space travel, try this delectable recipe of vegetable and shrimp pilaf made with red quinoa. This savory grain is similar to rice, wheat and barley and is a likely candidate for space food.

Unlike other plants, quinoa can survive the high ultraviolet radiation of space. The quinoa plant grows naturally high in the Andes, where the sun's ultraviolet rays are much stronger because of the thin atmosphere. The quinoa plant has evolved to be less susceptible to temperature variation, drought, pressure gradient and solar radiation.

Quinoa is high in nutrition and has been used as a grain for thousands of years in breads, soups, salads and pastries. If your local grocer doesn't have quinoa, most natural food stores will.

QUINOA (THE BASIC RECIPE)

1 cup quinoa

2 cups water

Rinse quinoa thoroughly with cold water before cooking. Drain excess water. Place quinoa and water in a large saucepan and bring to a boil. Reduce to a simmer, cover and cook until all of the water is absorbed (about 15 minutes). You will know that the quinoa is done when all of the grains have turned from white to transparent and the spiral-like grain has separated. Makes 3 cups.

Get creative by adding vegetables, fish, meat, spices, cheese, fruit, chocolate or whatever you have a taste for. On our spaceship, the quinoa would be served in a bowl and remain intact in zero-gravity with a thick, delicious sauce.

Quinoa was so sacred to the ancient Incas that each year the emperor used a golden spade to plant the first quinoa seeds of the season. At the solstice, Incan priests bearing golden vessels filled with quinoa made offerings to Inti, the Sun. Quinoa may be an excellent food for growing in space, because it has grown on Earth in such an extreme place.

Reality check: The Radiation Factor.

Radiation, and our inability to protect ourselves against it, may prove to be the biggest obstacle to long-duration space travel.

On Earth, our atmosphere forms a shield equivalent to a wall of lead three feet thick protecting us from solar radiation. On board *CosmicSea*, a thin reflective coating of gold foil on the ship's surface and an emergency bunker shields us from the dangerous radiation of solar storms. Lengthy stays on the Moon or Mars will require habitats shielded from solar radiation by thick berms of lunar or Martian soil.

Biosphere 2 is a 3.15-acre structure in Oracle, Arizona, designed to explore the complex web of life interactions and examine the potential for closed biospheres in space colonization. The project is a grand experiment in creating a sealed-off, self-sustaining ecosystem of the kind astronauts would need for lunar or Martian bases, or for extremely long trips into deep space. Biosphere 2 also provides insight about Earth's biosphere—Biosphere 1.

(FIGURE 86) BIOSPHERE 2. GILL KENNY, REPRINTED WITH PERMISSION OF GLOBAL ECOTECHNICS

A view of Earth's thin atmosphere from the International Space Station

(Figure 87) Ocean View. NASA

ALL FOR ONE AND ONE FOR ALL

Nature does not care if we live or die. Earth will do just fine without us. The continued existence of our human race is up to us. Humanity's ultimate survival depends on our interactions as individuals in a group.

Five centuries ago, systems thinker Leonardo da Vinci noted, "The earth is moved from its position by the weight of a tiny bird resting upon it."[3] Leonardo knew that small changes could create complex results. The butterfly effect, as it is currently called, loosely asserts that the flapping of a butterfly's wings in China could cause tiny atmospheric changes, which over a period of time could affect weather patterns in New York.

This intricate web of life is based upon the laws of the biosphere—the global ecological system integrating all living beings and their relationships with each other and the elements of Earth's atmosphere. These basic principles apply not only to butterflies, broccoli and hurricanes, but also to humans in everyday life. Global warming is just one example of how humans dramatically affect climate change on Earth.

The profound result of how we interact with our web of life is most obvious when we find ourselves in dire circumstances. Group behavior in extreme survival situations often requires an "all for one and one for all" attitude. In order to survive, group members need to share information, organize, plan and take action.

A good leader can help create a strong bond between members of a group by organizing their actions rather than having everyone act independently. Even though all members are equal and equally responsible for looking after themselves, a common plan inspired by a strong leader is key to survival.

Everyday Travel Tip
KNOW THE RULES OF THE RAFT

How we interact in CosmicSea's biosphere could be guided by the two rules of the raft. These two aspects of human behavior were experienced by Dr. Alain Bombard in 1952 when he spent five months with four castaways on a raft in the Indian Ocean "without succumbing to the urge to kill."[4]

Bombard's experience was self-imposed. He put himself and his men on a raft in the open ocean because he wanted to show that rescue attempts at sea should not be abandoned in only ten days; that men could survive in decent shape living off the resources of the sea—by eating plankton, squeezing fresh water out of fish flesh and even drinking some seawater (a practice not advised by survivalist John "Lofty" Wiseman[5]). Bombard and his fellow survivors managed to avoid even a "serious dispute" by interacting on the following two principles.

1. Each person is responsible for the welfare of the whole group.

2. Survival depends on the total cooperation of all on board.

This kind of cooperation, commitment and interaction between people is necessary whether they are on a raft, in a spaceship or in a village on planet Earth.

Alain Bombard on the cover of an old issue of *Mon Journal*

(FIGURE 88) BOMBARD. *MON JOURNAL*

Reality check: We may not always find ourselves in dire straits with cooperative people. If selfish behavior begins to destroy your chances for survival, then the other rule of the raft may apply: "Fend for yourself." Good luck.

YOUR SIX DEGREES OF SEPARATION

A theory known as the "six degrees of separation" postulates that everyone in the world is connected to everyone else through a path of six people or fewer. This interconnectedness means that our individual actions can affect the welfare of the whole group.

Movie buffs have long recognized the six degrees of separation theory in a game where you have to connect any given actor to actor Kevin Bacon. It's now clear that the six degrees game works because Kevin Bacon can be linked to Charlie Chaplin in just three steps, through films starring Laurence Fishburne and Marlon Brando.

The six degrees of separation theory postulates that everyone in the world is connected to everyone else through a path of six people or fewer.

(Figure 89) Six Degrees. Space Traveler, Inc.

Going a step further, what does Hollywood actor Kevin Bacon have in common with you and me? All of us have been linked by a mathematical theory called the "small world effect,"[6] in which apparently unrelated people turn out to have friends in common. This small world effect helps us understand a wide range of phenomena—from the way disease spreads, to global monetary fluctuations, to what makes hit songs.

All that's needed for the small world effect is for a tiny proportion of interconnections to link up with distant parts of the network. A small world model of infections reveals that a few people can dramatically spread disease by crossing social or geographical boundaries. You don't need to know any of these people personally to be connected to a high-risk group. On a more positive note, you don't need to know any of the people who may benefit from your next invention, good deed or inspiring words.

Everyday Travel Tip
MAKING WAVES

Toss a stone into a still pond or a bar of soap into a bathtub of still water. Water ripples out in a series of widening circles. Now toss two stones and then three or more. Observe the patterns and connections. How does one ripple affect another? Where does the energy of the ripples go?

Next, experiment with drawing a diagram that represents the interconnections of your personal web of life. With you at the center, use lines and circles to connect your family, friends, business associates, corporations and larger segments of society. How can you enhance your "ripple effect" on others?

The ripple effect
(FIGURE 90) RIPPLE EFFECT.
"JUGGLING"— COPYRIGHT
(C) 2006, MARTIN WAUGH,
WWW.LIQUIDSCULPTURE.COM

ACCEPTING EACH OTHER'S DIFFERENCES

"Imagine taking a trip cross country with your family," says Marc Shepanek, a psychologist who worked as NASA's manager of aerospace medicine. "Now imagine that it lasts for months on end. And that you can't open the windows. You can't even get out of the car. The bathroom and the meals are in the car with you. Think there might be a problem getting along?"[7]

Long-duration space missions will require people with balanced psychological profiles. The last astronaut aboard the Russian *Mir* space station, Andy Thomas, says each space traveler will "have to be strong enough to deal with what you perceive as not imperfections, but differences between you and them."

A Russian proverb, told years ago by cosmonaut Oleg Atkov, states that "individuals should never undertake a difficult and risky task until they had consumed together 20 kg of salt." The obvious interpretation is that people should share many meals together and get to know each other's similarities and differences well before they embark on a long journey.

Fifth Insight
INTERACTING WITH THE BIOSPHERE

Whether we are living within the fragile biosphere of Earth or balancing the life-support systems of a spacecraft, our interactions with each other and our environment affect the complex web of life that keeps us alive. One person's actions can impact everyone else.

Use the interconnectedness of all things to succeed in your daily life. Create meaningful networks of people, places and things. Respect each other's differences by recognizing the similarities.

Be a responsible crewmember on spaceship Earth. Survival depends on the cooperation of all on board. If we can't live together, we may die alone.

This montage features the International Space Station and the culturally diverse crew of the Space Shuttle *Columbia* STS-107: David M. Brown, Rick Husband, Laurel Clark, Kalpana Chawla, Michael P. Anderson, William McCool and Ilan Ramon.

On February 1, 2003, the Space Shuttle *Columbia* disintegrated as it tried to reenter the Earth's atmosphere after a 16-day mission in space. All seven members of the multicultural crew were lost: six Americans, one Israeli. Three were seasoned astronauts; four were on their first space flight. Among the scientists, surgeons and a fighter pilot were an African-American man and the first Indian-American astronaut.

(FIGURE 91) ISS STS-107 CREW. NASA

Author's Log
MIDNIGHT, JULY 8, 2099—THE POINT OF NO RETURN

In a few short hours, we will leave geosynchronous orbit around Earth and begin our voyage through interplanetary space.

On the way to Mars, we must live our lives in balance with the ship's biosphere. Anyone's selfish, shortsighted indulgence could foul the ship's life-support system and destroy all of us before ever finding LifePoint.

There's no turning back now. We have only one way to go—but go we must. From here, our destination is a distant red speck in the black vastness of space. The mystery remains. Will we find life?

If all of civilization can find a common focus, then perhaps wars, poverty and pollution might be avoided on Earth. When the enemy of humankind is man himself, then maybe pursuing humanity's survival in space can be a substitute for the battles that destroy eachother on Earth.

Our destination, Mars, is in clear view out this porthole—magnified several times by the changeable optical properties of the glass.
(FIGURE 92) BIOSPHERE PORT. SPACE TRAVELER, INC.

It's your web of life. Who can you connect to, now and in the future?

(FIGURE 93) YOUR WEB. SPACE TRAVELER, INC.

CosmicSea leaves Earth's orbit. We're on our way to Mars.

(Figure 94) *CosmicSea* Leaves. Space Traveler, Inc.

CHAPTER SIX

Focusing on a Journeystar

The greatest thing in this world
is not so much where we are,
but in what direction we are
moving.

———

OLIVER WENDELL HOLMES, writer/poet
(1809 – 1894)

Author's Log
EARLY MORNING, JULY 9, 2099—HEADING TO MARS

This morning we were gently nudged awake by the ignition of rockets blasting us to
Mars. *CosmicSea* is now speeding out of Earth's orbit toward a rendezvous with the
Red Planet.

As we pass by the Moon, Earth becomes a constantly shrinking blue dot in the deep-
ening distance. This leg of our journey will take five months, so we might as well sit
back and enjoy the ride.

Because Earth and Mars are in two different orbits around the Sun, we are aiming for
a point in space where Mars *will be* by the time we get there. It's like throwing a dart
at a moving dartboard. We have to hit our target with absolute certainty. If we travel
past the grip of Martian gravity, *CosmicSea* and all of us on board will be slingshot far
beyond our destination.

We deploy the ship's solar sail and find solace in its massive size and power. Filled
with the energy of countless light photons, our solar sail propels us like a boat's sail
filled with a strong wind on the high sea—comforting us in the same way the *May-
flower*'s sails did for the Pilgrims. The mirror image of our ship in the reflective sail is
a constant reminder that we are travelers on an incredible voyage through star-filled
space. As we tune this great golden sail, the power of focused light propels us even
faster.

FINDING OUR FOCUS

LEONARDO DA VINCI ONCE SAID: **"He who fixes his course to a star does not change his mind."** To get anywhere in life we have to have a destination, a point of focus, and then chart a course to get there. Focusing on our goal empowers our every action, making our dreams realities using the laws of attraction.

Whether we're charting our course to Mars or planning our lives on Earth, we need to know where we want to go and stay focused on the goal—be it a lighthouse on the horizon, a planet in space or a vision for our life.

Because our physical destination is a moving target, we must propel *CosmicSea* in the right direction at the right time so that we arrive at a point in space when the orbiting planet Mars will be there. Like throwing a dart at a moving target, we'll have to lead the aim point by just the right amount. It's a matter of timing and speed down to a tiny fraction of a millimeter per second. If we don't account for the force of the solar wind, we could be off by over two miles (3.5 km) in just ten days.

To navigate a spacecraft like *CosmicSea* to Mars, we need to know two things: how far the spaceship is from Earth and its location in space. NASA can locate spaceships that send a time-coded signal to at least two of the three radio telescopes on Earth at the same time. The Deep Space Network (DSN), as it's called, currently consists of three radio telescopes placed approximately 120 degrees apart, or one-third of the way around Earth. This positioning ensures that there is always at least one telescope that can send and receive signals facing any point in space at any time.

Using the Deep Space Network, we can compare how far a spaceship is from any two radio telescopes and any another known object in space, like a bright star or a nebula. Using the three locations—two telescopes and a star—a technique called triangulation helps us calculate a spaceship's location.

We use the same triangulation technique every day to locate our position on Earth. If your car has a GPS, or Global Positioning Satellite system, then you are triangulating with satellites orbiting high above your head to locate your destination.

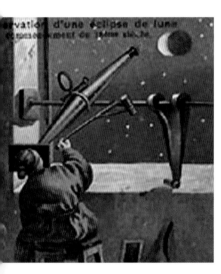

Renaissance Man
looking through telescope
(FIGURE 95) RENAISSANCE MAN.
ANONYMOUS

A Deep Space Network radio telescope at Goldstone, in California

(Figure 96) Radio Telescope. Jet Propulsion Laboratory

FINDING OUR WAY EVERY DAY

What if we find ourselves lost somewhere on Earth without a GPS system to help us? How do we find our way? Well, like humans have done for thousands of years, we can always use the closest star in the sky, our Sun, as our guide.

Everyone knows that the Sun rises from the east and sets in the west. Less well known is that almost everything in the sky—including the Moon, planets and most of the stars—also rises from the east and sets in the west. This is the major movement of objects in the sky and is due to the rotation of Earth. Because the Sun rises from the east and sets in the west, shadows are a good means of triangulating both direction and time of day.

Triangulation determines a spacecraft's location from two radio telescopes on Earth and a fixed point in space such as a distant star. Triangulating determines our position, whether we're in our car using a GPS or in a spacecraft like *CosmicSea*.

(FIGURE 97) TRIANGULATION. SPACE TRAVELER, INC.

> **Everyday Travel Tip**
> **THE SHADOW KNOWS THE WAY**
>
> Use a shadow stick to determine direction. Place a three-foot-long stick as upright as possible on a patch of flat, clear ground. Mark with a pebble the spot where the tip of the shadow falls. Wait at least 15 minutes and mark the new shadow tip. Joining the two points will give the direction of east and west—the first mark is west. North-south will be at right angles to this line. At its highest point in the sky, the Sun is due south in the northern hemisphere.
>
> The shadow stick method works at any time of day when there is sunshine and at any latitude.[1] Use it for spot checks on your way out of unexplored territory.

CELESTIAL NAVIGATION

Fortunately for us, the cars, planes and ships we travel in on Earth are guided by sophisticated satellite positioning systems. Ancient travelers, on the other hand, had their own sophisticated system for finding their way on Earth—celestial navigation: the ancient art and science of finding your way by the stars, Sun, Moon and planets.

The basic theory behind celestial navigation is: find your unknown position from a known position. If we have some information, we can deduce the rest. On Earth's northern hemisphere, the North Star has been the primary reference point for explorers for thousands of years.

Ancient seafarers navigated with confidence over thousands of miles of empty ocean using no compasses, charts, sextants or GPS systems. They used the stars. They looked upon celestial navigation not merely as a technique of getting from one island to another but as a way of life.

In the same way, on Expedition LifePoint, we use celestial navigation not because we have to, but because the sheer act of focusing on a specific star gives us a visual reference point and an inner sense of direction on our personal journey.

The greatest ancient navigators combined philosophy and spirituality. They were held in high esteem and considered great leaders of society. These ancient explorers knew the sky the same way we know the faces of the people we love.

Whether we're traveling to an island in the ocean or a distant planet in space, knowing our direction of travel can get us to our destination quickly and safely. Developing a good sense of direction on Earth can foster a solid direction in life.

Polaris is the nearest bright star to the north spin axis of Earth. Therefore, as Earth turns, stars appear to rotate around Polaris, making it the North Star. As Earth spins on its axis every 24 hours, all the other stars in the sky seem to move around the North Star, which does not appear to move. On long-exposure photographs, stars form circular paths around the sky, and the North Star remains in the center of the circles, unmoving. The stars only appear to stay in the same positions related to one another and pass over the same places on Earth night after night because they are so far away and our lives are too short to perceive their motion. In reality, those stars are speeding along at 100,000 miles per hour within their own galaxies. Their passage over the horizon starts four minutes earlier each night due to our orbit around the Sun. The North Star's height above the horizon, in degrees, is also your latitude.

Polaris has not always been the North Star and won't be in the future. The rotational axis of Earth slowly changes direction, in a circle, over thousands of years. Currently it points within one degree of Polaris. During the past 5,000 years, the axis has pointed at the star Thuban (Alpha Draconis); in the year 7500, the North Star will be Alpha Cephei; in the year 15000 it will be the star Vega. About 9,000 years after that, Polaris will again become the North Star.

Is there a corresponding star in the skies of the southern hemisphere that travelers can use to find due south? Unfortunately, there is no such star. The rotational axis of Earth is currently pointing at a section of the sky that contains no stars bright enough to be seen easily by the naked eye. Instead, navigators make use of a constellation called the Southern Cross.

(FIGURE 98) NORTH STAR. WALLY PACHOLKA

THE POWER OF FOCUS

Once we know our location, making headway requires focusing energy on our destination. Focused energy creates tremendous power.

For example, calm air can become a deadly force when focused into the funnel of a tornado. Tranquil ocean water on a calm sunny day can become a destructive force when focused into a single tsunami wave. In the same way, light focused into a laser beam can be used to perform delicate eye surgery, guide rockets and even propel spacecraft.

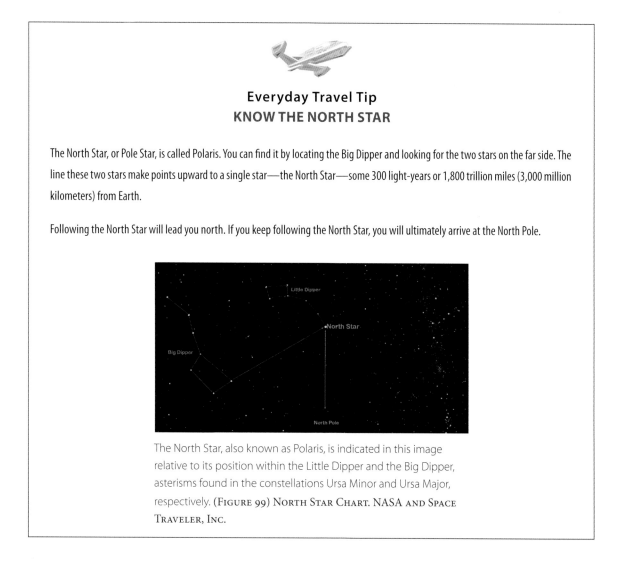

Everyday Travel Tip
KNOW THE NORTH STAR

The North Star, or Pole Star, is called Polaris. You can find it by locating the Big Dipper and looking for the two stars on the far side. The line these two stars make points upward to a single star—the North Star—some 300 light-years or 1,800 trillion miles (3,000 million kilometers) from Earth.

Following the North Star will lead you north. If you keep following the North Star, you will ultimately arrive at the North Pole.

The North Star, also known as Polaris, is indicated in this image relative to its position within the Little Dipper and the Big Dipper, asterisms found in the constellations Ursa Minor and Ursa Major, respectively. (FIGURE 99) NORTH STAR CHART. NASA AND SPACE TRAVELER, INC.

SOLAR SAILING

Nearly 400 years ago, while others were still traveling the oceans aboard wooden sailing ships, Johannes Kepler proposed the idea of exploring the galaxy using sails filled with light. After observing that comet tails were blown around by some kind of solar breeze, Kepler believed sails could capture that solar wind and propel spacecraft just as winds moved ships on the seas.[2] Thanks to Kepler, today's scientists are beginning to design solar sail spacecraft that are pushed through the cosmos by light.

Light is basically a stream of photons—mass-less particles of energy traveling in a wave-like pattern at the speed of light. Light is a form of electromagnetic energy that exerts force on objects it comes in contact with. When deployed, *CosmicSea*'s super-thin reflective solar sail catches the energy of light particles in the same way a fabric sail catches the force of the wind.

Thanks to the additional power of light in *CosmicSea*'s solar sails, our travel time to Mars will be several weeks shorter than the 180 days or so that a fast conjunction trajectory[3] would take using only chemical propulsion systems. Comparably speaking, our journey will be shorter than the first journeys of immigrants who set sail to America from Europe in the 19th century.

A solar sail spacecraft doesn't need tanks of heavy liquid fuel launched from Earth's gravity well. The Sun provides the fuel.

A spacecraft propelled by sunlight can build up speeds that rocket-powered vehicles could never achieve. A solar sail spacecraft could potentially travel at 200,000 miles per hour. That is ten times faster than the Space Shuttle's orbital speed of 17,500 miles per hour. To give you an idea how fast that is, you could travel from New York to Los Angeles in less than a minute. However, to become a practical means of space travel, solar sail–powered spacecraft will need an additional push from microwave or laser light beams on Earth, in orbit or a trailing satellite.

Solar sails have great potential for interstellar travel. Famed science fiction writer Arthur C. Clarke envisioned an entire regatta of space-sailing craft in his collection of short stories titled *The Wind from the Sun*. Future Olympics may one day include a Solar Cup—a sailing competition for spaceships powered by light from the Sun.

Oil painting of Johannes Kepler circa 1620 by an unknown artist. Kepler became a follower of Copernicus. He later worked with Tycho Brahe in Prague, where he worked out the orbit of Mars. This led him to discover the laws of planetary motion. Kepler was also influential in the evolution of infinitesimal calculus.

(FIGURE 100) KEPLER. ARTIST UNKNOWN

Although it looks like a flying saucer from an old science fiction movie, this scale-model spacecraft, developed by Leik Myrabo at the Rensselaer Polytechnic Institute in New Mexico, is actually being propelled into the air on a beam of focused laser light. The energy from the photons of focused light lifts the craft like wind filling the sails of a ship. (FIGURE 101) LIGHTCRAFT. RENSSELAER POLYTECHNIC INSTITUTE, WHITE SANDS, NEW MEXICO

NAVIGATING LIFE WITH A JOURNEYSTAR

Life is a journey. As with any journey, if we don't have a strategy, map or plan, we may get lost.

If we are lost somewhere on the planet's surface, we are wise to make a map of our surrounding terrain. Depending on where we are, we might climb a tree to get a better view and note the contours of the land, the rivers, streams, isolated trees and other prominent

CosmicSea under solar sail on Expedition LifePoint. The large solar sail is propelled forward by photons of light hitting it. The reflection of Earth grows smaller as we travel farther and farther from home.

(FIGURE 102) *CosmicSea* SAILS. NASA/PLANETARY SOCIETY AND SPACE TRAVELER, INC.

landmarks. If we can't see everything before us, we can make a map with blank spots and fill them with information as we explore. With a map, we can plan our way forward.

Having a map for our lives is equally important. A life plan is a valuable tool that can guide us every day.

Like the ancient explorers of Earth who focused on the North Star to guide their journeys, or the space explorers of today who find their way between planets using the latest satellite navigation systems, we too can chart our course in life with a clear vision, a plan and the right tools. We can find our way in almost any situation by focusing on a star in the sky or a symbolic star in the vision of our lives.

"There is a time for departure even when there's no certain place to go," wrote playwright Tennessee Williams. Like the characters in his plays, sometimes we simply have to follow our hearts even if we have no particular destination in mind. Doing what we are passionate about can guide us every day and lead us in a positive direction.

Clearly, we can't go in two directions at once. We ultimately must chose one direction or the other and deal with the consequences. By making a sacrifice, we are actually taking a step in our new direction. But enter the dark forest, swamp or the vast unknown we must, or else stay right where we are and never get anywhere.

Many people focus their thoughts either on what they don't want or on reinforcing what they're already getting. Instead, keep your thoughts focused on what you desire. Like the physical law of attraction uses the power of gravity to pull objects toward each other, the mental law of attraction uses the power of focus to attract what we want in life.

Ships and sails proper for the heavenly air should be fashioned. Then there will also be people, who do not shrink from the dreary vastness of space.

———

Johannes Kepler, German astronomer (1571 – 1630)

Sixth Insight
FOCUSING ON A JOURNEYSTAR

During my first flying lesson above the cornfields of Iowa, a stunt pilot known as Upside-Down Henry told me to "focus on the place to land, not on the place you could crash."

He was right. Focus on what you want, not on what you don't want.

Our focus is our reality; it gives us direction. If you become lost, confused or disoriented, focus on immediate solutions and strategies. Take one step at a time.

Focusing helps us to survive and thrive. Expedition LifePoint's goal of landing safely on Mars creates a common focus for all humans on Earth.

In your daily life, focus your time and energy on doing the things you are truly brilliant at. Create a powerful personal compass for finding your way in life by triangulating your purpose, your passion and your proof so they converge on a single point of focus—a journeystar.

This painting depicts an abbreviated evolution of spaceships leading to the ultimate exploration of Mars.

(FIGURE 103) AURORA. EUROPEAN SPACE AGENCY

Author's Log
EARLY MORNING—FIVE MONTHS LATER
NOVEMBER 30, 2099—ENTERING MARTIAN SKIES

This morning I woke early to the blast of retrorockets as *CosmicSea* reversed position and decelerated into orbit around Mars. I didn't sleep much anyway. There's been no "day" or "night" per se on our five-month journey across interplanetary space. I'm anxious to land on solid ground even if it isn't Earth.

Although comfortable, the accommodations on board *CosmicSea* have been tight and the isolation trying. We are all looking forward to setting foot on the Red Planet tomorrow and waking up to our first Martian sunrise. It will be a wonderful treat to see some new faces—the brave pioneers of the first human colony on Mars, New Shangri-la.

In the next few hours, we must prepare to land on the surface of another planet and begin our search for other life. What we discover on Mars may ensure a future for humans on Earth.

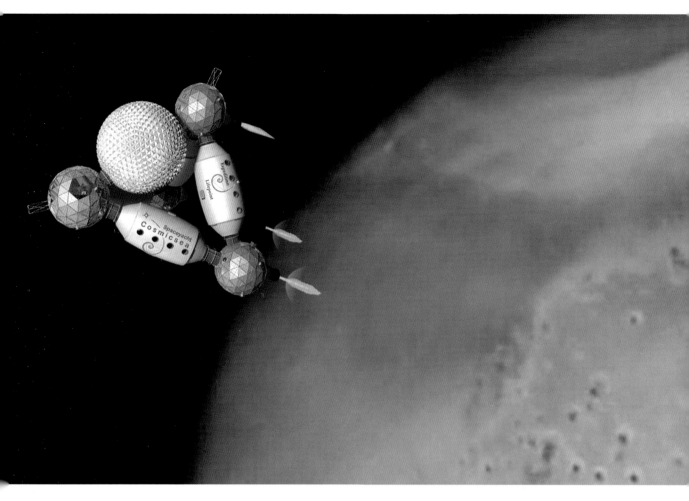

CosmicSea reverses position and heads tail-first toward Mars. Retrorocket thrust from the Powerspheres slows our speed from over 20,000 miles per hour to 1,900 miles per hour. If the retro-burn fails, our spacecraft will continue to fly on past the planet. If all goes well, *CosmicSea* will gradually enter a tightly bound, elliptical orbit around Mars. Soon, we'll board our landing craft, *LifeLander,* for the dangerous trip to the Martian surface.

(FIGURE 104) *CosmicSea* RETROS. SPACE TRAVELER, INC.

DISCOVERING

It is good to have an end to journey toward;
but it is the journey that matters, in the end.

———

Ursula K. Le Guin, writer (1929 –)

CosmicSea reverses position, performs a retrorocket burn and gradually enters an orbit around Mars. Protected by an outer heat shield capsule, *LifeLander* and its passengers enter the Martian atmosphere for a dramatic ride to the surface.

(FIGURE 105) *LIFELANDER*. SPACE TRAVELER, INC.

CHAPTER SEVEN

Living to Thrive

There is life on Mars.
And it is us. It is us.

———

RAY BRADBURY, writer (1920 –)

Author's Log
MORNING, DECEMBER 1, 2099 (EARTH TIME)
LANDING ON MARS

If traveling to Mars has been dangerous, I think that landing here will be even riskier. The entry, descent and touchdown may only take six minutes, but the ride is going to be intense. If we arrive alive, we will need to survive over a year on the surface before we begin our journey back home.

Safely secured inside our landing craft, *LifeLander*, we are jettisoned from *CosmicSea*'s rear deck and begin to drop quickly toward the surface of Mars.

LifeLander slows our descent to less than 200 miles per hour as it aero-brakes in the thin atmosphere. We're counting on the outer heat shield to protect us from soaring temperatures and a fiery death.

With only two minutes until landing, at the altitude of an airliner on Earth, a parachute deploys and further slows our descent. The heat shield releases and falls to the surface beneath us.

Over the next two minutes, we descend through the orange-colored sky toward the rocky red landscape below. Out the windows we see unfamiliar terrain, barren and hostile, with strange similarities to the deserts of America's Southwest.

LifeLander's parachute opens over the
Martian North Pole as the heat shield
is jettisoned and falls to the surface first.
(Figure 106) *LifeLander* Chute.
NASA and Space Traveler, Inc.

At New Shangri-la, we join other explorers
in the search for life on Mars.
(Figure 107) New Shangri-la.
Space Traveler, Inc.

Just 20 seconds before touchdown, our landing rockets ignite with a flash. In a matter of seconds, we slow to a mere ten miles per hour only 40 feet above the ground. With a solid thump, we finally touch down on a crude landing pad near a small village of domed structures.

Once again, life lands on Mars. This outpost of humanity on another planet may be nicknamed New Shangri-la, but this tiny settlement is far from a perfect utopia.

We step out of *LifeLander* and onto the surface of this new world. Our legs are a little wobbly but the subtle Martian gravity is a welcome relief after floating for so long in weightlessness. The feeling is comparable to standing on firm ground after a lengthy voyage at sea.

Through the reddish haze, we can see the horizon, noticeably closer than the horizon on Earth. A pressurized Mars Utility Vehicle (MUV) lumbers over a nearby dune. It is a relief to see a human sitting in the driver's seat, coming to take us to our home away from home— the first Mars Base Biosphere near the North Pole's frozen spiral landscape.

As we enter the Rover, small remote cameras on and in the vehicle capture our every move and remind us that people back home are vicariously joining our search for other life in the universe. The communication time lag of eight minutes with people back on Earth is part of daily life for the six men and women living here and anxiously awaiting our arrival.

Only three previous expedition teams have set foot on this 4-billion-year-old world. They all survived the journey, made the most of their resources, lived and thrived on another world. There is life on Mars. Human life!

As we drive toward our new home in the middle of this small complex of domes, the seventh insight begins to sink in. Don't just survive. Thrive!

THE LIFE ON MARS IS US

WE HUMANS LANDED THE FIRST VIKING SPACECRAFT on Mars July 20, 1976. The morning after, a TV interviewer asked renowned science fiction author Ray Bradbury a poignant question. The interviewer said, "Mr. Bradbury, you've been writing about life on Mars all of your life. Now the first photographs have come through, and there is no life on Mars. How do you feel about that?"

Bradbury's answer was, "Fool! There is life on Mars. And it is us."[1]

The two Viking landers and other robotic probes—Sojourner, Spirit, Opportunity and Phoenix—sitting on the Martian surface today are indisputable evidence that human life has touched another planet, albeit remotely. Even though the instruments on board Phoenix didn't find life in a few scoopfuls of Martian sand, it does not rule out the possibility of life lurking elsewhere—perhaps just a few feet beneath the surface in frozen permafrost.

IN LIKENESS OF EARTH

The physical properties of Mars, the fourth planet from the Sun, are strikingly similar to those on Earth, the third planet from the Sun. A Martian day, or sol, is only 37 minutes longer than the 24-hour day on Earth. A Martian year, however, lasts 687 Earth days; almost twice as long as a year on Earth. Both planets are tilted on their axis to a similar degree and cause a change of seasons. Many plants grown on Earth today could likely adapt to these Martian seasons inside a greenhouse and feed the travelers and settlers who choose to live there.

Ice on Mars's Utopia Planitia. This high-resolution color photo of the surface of Mars was taken by Viking Lander 2 at its Utopia Planitia landing site on May 18, 1979, and relayed to Earth by Viking Orbiter 1. There is a sparse coating of water ice on the rocks and soil, no more than a thousandth of an inch thick.

The thin Martian atmosphere consists of 95% carbon dioxide, which freezes in winter, adheres to the dust particles in the air and becomes heavy enough to sink to the ground. Warmed by the Sun, the surface evaporates the carbon dioxide and returns it to the atmosphere, leaving behind the water and dust. The footpad of the Viking 2 lander is visible in the lower right corner of the image.

(FIGURE 108) MARS FROST. NASA/JPL

During Martian winters, white clouds high in the atmosphere cloak the North and South Poles.
(FIGURE 109) MARS CLOUDS. NASA/JPL

This early NASA artwork envisions humans' first landing on Mars.
(FIGURE 110) FIRST LANDING. NASA

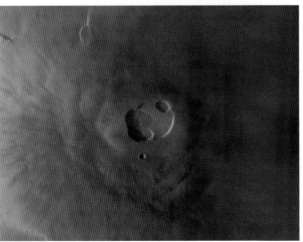

This image of Olympus Mons, the Prince of the Solar System, was taken from an altitude of 310 kilometers above Mars in 1997 on a beautiful October afternoon. Note the presence of water clouds at the summit.
(FIGURE 111) OLYMPUS MONS. NASA/JPL

Olympus Mons is three times as tall as Mount Everest—almost 15 miles—making it the largest volcano in our solar system. (FIGURE 112) OLYMPUS MONS SIDE. NASA/JPL

There are also a few striking differences between Earth and Mars. The highest known mountain in the solar system is the Martian volcano Olympus Mons, three times higher than Earth's Mount Everest. Olympus Mons towers 78,000 feet, almost 15 miles (24 kilometers) above the planet's cold and dry surface. The planet has a thin atmosphere of mostly carbon dioxide due to the lack of one cohesive magnetic field like we have on Earth.

Earth's single magnetic field is generated by its fluid molten core and helps hold our breathable atmosphere in place. Over millions of years, Mars's molten core solidified and fragmented into many smaller magnetic fields. The breakdown of the magnetic field's cohesive nature probably took the Martian biosphere with it, blown away by the solar wind.

Since Mars is smaller than Earth, Martian gravity is about one-third of what we experience here. Plants and people may actually become taller on Mars because of the lower gravity. And what fun we'll have jumping for joy higher than we ever could on Earth!

Mounting geologic evidence suggests that Mars once had a warm, wet environment potentially friendly to life. Discovering life, or even fossils of past Martian life, would dramatically increase the chance that life abounds in the universe. Finding life on Mars would provide proof that other planets in our cosmic sea may indeed teem with plants, creatures and brand-new life forms.

This topographic portrayal shows Mars as it might have looked midway through its history, according to the oceans hypothesis. The northern lowlands are occupied by an ocean. The Tharsis region, with numerous, very large shield volcanoes, is seen in the central part of the globe. In the upper right, many channels flow into the northern lowlands at Chryse Planitia.

(FIGURE 113) MARS OCEAN. NASA MARS GLOBAL SURVEYOR PROJECT; MOLA TEAM. RENDERING BY PETER NEIVERT, BROWN UNIVERSITY

This image of Mars was taken by the Viking 1 spacecraft in 1975. White cloud cover is visible around the towering volcanoes and the North Pole near the site of New Shangri-la.

(FIGURE 114) NEW SHANGRI-LA SITE. NASA AND SPACE TRAVELER, INC.

ALIENS ON EARTH

Life is not always easy to define. Basically, if it eats nutrients, uses energy, reproduces and secretes waste, then it's alive.

Every day, scientists right here on Earth search for life—and find life—in places where we'd least expect it. In the harsh Mars-like environments of the Canadian Arctic, astrobiologists are discovering 30,000-year-old bacteria hibernating in subterranean permafrost that come to life when warmed under a microscope. In the coldest, deepest parts of Earth's oceans, thriving in warm waters surrounding sub-sea volcanic vents, explorers are finding bizarre, never-seen-before giant clams, crabs that glow and enormous dandelion-shaped sea creatures.

The oceans of Earth are full of wondrous creatures unlike anything we have yet to discover in the wilderness of space. Personal encounters with creatures of the seas can be out of this world.

I'll never forget scuba diving at night with a dozen giant manta rays 40 feet deep in the Pacific Ocean off the coast of Hawaii. I became a participant in a surreal three-dimensional ballet performed by these graceful underwater giants with wingspans larger than me. As I stabilized myself between two large rocks on the ocean bottom, these ancient creatures of the deep flew synchronized looping patterns, taking turns coming straight toward me with their giant mouths agape, scooping up the bountiful plankton attracted by my flashlight. Like gentle flying dinosaurs, the rays would swoop over my head and gently brush against me with their giant bodies, but never with the intent to harm.

Floating weightless with these spaceship-shaped creatures in the water world is truly a space experience—as is any underwater encounter with dolphins, whales, sharks, jellyfish, lobsters and even tiny bioluminescent phytoplankton.

A manta ray can grow to
12 feet in width and
gracefully glide through
the oceans in search of prey.
(FIGURE 115) MANTA RAY. RAINBOW DIVERS

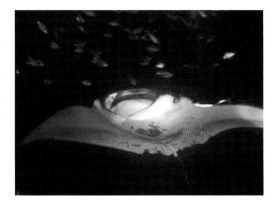

Under the Antarctic ice, a jellyfish species, *Diplulmaris antarctica,* floats
with the current just offshore of McMurdo Station, Ross Island. Its
colorless umbrella can be up to 8 inches in diameter.
(FIGURE 116) JELLYFISH. STEVE CLABUESCH, NATIONAL SCIENCE
FOUNDATION

The shape of the spacecraft in H.G. Wells' *The War of the Worlds* has a
strong resemblance to the manta rays living in Earth's oceans.
(FIGURE 117) *WAR OF THE WORLDS.* GEORGE PAL

IS ANYBODY OUT THERE?

Some 2,000 years ago, Greek philosopher Metrodorus of Chios wrote, "It is unnatural in a large field to have only one shaft of wheat, and in the infinite Universe only one living world." Still, life must have overcome significant odds to be created out of stardust on the third planet from our Sun.

If other life exists in the universe, what is it like? Is it simple like the green scum floating on the pond in the park, or squid-like creatures swimming beneath the frozen seas of Jupiter's moon Europa or winged-aliens flying high in the gas clouds of Jupiter? Are they smart techno-savvy, two-legged green-eyed creatures with oversized heads and long skinny arms? Do they have families like you and I do?

What is the likelihood of other life in the universe developing **intelligence**? Some argue that intelligent life is a billion-to-one shot and happened only once on Earth. Without proof, the possibility remains that our fragile planet could be the singular beginning of life in the universe—or the end of it.

My guess is that some form of life exists on other planets in the cosmos. Based upon the number of stars in the sky, some have calculated that there must be at least 100 billion planets suitable for life in the known universe.

The late astronomer Carl Sagan once estimated that there were potentially thousands of technological civilizations in our galaxy alone. The Drake equation[2] concludes that there could be as many as

Everyday Travel Tip
HAVE A CLOSE ENCOUNTER

Have a close encounter with a unique creature of Earth in a safe and humane situation. Gently coax a butterfly onto your finger in your backyard, whistle back to a bird singing in the forest or swim with dolphins in the wild blue sea. View life from that creature's eyes and get a new perspective on your own life.

50,000 planets with advanced civilizations in our Milky Way Galaxy. That means that only one in a million stars might have a detectable civilization. So far it seems, in the mere 50 years we've been listening, we have not been in the right place at the right time to pick up that first radio transmission from another intelligent civilization.

MIRACLES AND MARTIANS?

Simple life forms appeared quite early in Earth's history, at a time when Mars was a more habitable planet. It's quite possible that an asteroid impact with Mars may have blasted primitive, tiny organisms living deep inside Martian bedrock to Earth, sparking life on our planet as we know it today. (Or, perhaps a rock from Earth seeded life on Mars.) Rocks from Mars make it to Earth at the rate of almost half a ton per year. If life did hitchhike to Earth from Mars, then we may very well be descendants of Martians.[3]

But what if we find that Mars never produced any life, despite its history of flowing rivers? Then the evolution of life may be rare indeed—a solitary spark in the great cosmic sea. Without proof, we'll continue to live with the current knowledge that we might be all alone in the universe.

The latest photographs of Jupiter's moon Europa from NASA's *Galileo* spacecraft have led scientists to believe in the possibility of an ocean that could be over 60 miles deep in some places and sustain life forms that are warmed by underwater geothermal vents and volcanoes. Imagine being a creature on a planet completely covered in water and whose "sky" is a thick layer of ice! (FIGURE 118) EUROPA. NASA

In this sense, life could be viewed as either a mere coincidence or a miracle. After all, what is a miracle but a stroke of luck—a more-or-less improbable natural event that actually occurs? "Nothing is too wonderful to be true, if it be consistent with the laws of nature," wrote 18th-century physicist Michael Faraday.

Galaxies of deep space. To capture this unprecedented image of a massive cluster of yellowish galaxies, the Hubble Space Telescope peered straight through the center of one of the most massive galaxy clusters known, called *Abell 1689*. The gravity of the cluster's trillion stars—plus dark matter—acts as a 2-million-light-year-wide "lens" in space. This "gravitational lens" bends and magnifies the light of the galaxies located far behind it. Some of the faintest objects in the picture may be over 13 billion light-years away. (**Figure 119**) Deep Space. NASA/ESA

Men are weak now,
and yet they transform
the Earth's surface.
In millions of years
their might will increase
to the extent that
they will change
the surface of the Earth,
its oceans, the atmosphere,
and themselves.
They will control the climate
and the Solar System
just as they control the Earth.
They will travel beyond the
limits of our planetary system;
they will reach other Suns…

——

Konstantin Tsiolkovsky, space
visionary (1857 – 1935)

ARE WE FUTURE MARTIANS?

We first sent men to the Moon in 1969 and returned them safely home. Once we put our minds to it, we'll send humans to Mars. Our initial forays will be temporary, but eventually we'll establish permanent settlements.

Some scientists think we could ultimately transform Mars into a more Earth-like world. Using the same technologies that have caused global warming and made the atmosphere on Earth to be more like Mars—inhospitable—it seems likely that we could deliberately alter Mars's biosphere with a comparable process known as terraforming.[4] This kind of planetary engineering could potentially bring life to a planet that has all the chemical elements needed for life—carbon, nitrogen, hydrogen and oxygen.

Today, it's obvious that we are far from being able to understand and control the climate of our own planet. Changing the climate of an entire barren planet to a shirt-sleeved environment for humans is a tough thing to do and unlikely in the foreseeable future. In the short term, we can more easily make Mars livable by building networks of greenhouses and enclosed homes for early travelers. All the resources to make plastics and glass are readily available right there on Mars.

An image of Konstantin Tsiolkovsky was featured with a space station on a Romanian postage stamp in 1988. (Figure 120) Tsiolkovsky. CPA/USSR

While the Wright Brothers were still building bicycles, Konstantin Tsiolkovsky, a space visionary in Russia, outlined a strategy for populating the galaxy. By the middle of the 1920s, Tsiolkovsky believed that surviving in space would require, among other things, that we:

(1) Build, test and fly winged airplanes powered by rocket engines such as the X-15 in 1963 and *SpaceShipOne* in 2004.

(2) Learn to grow plants in space, creating food and a breathable atmosphere in habitats that can sustain human life.

(3) Populate the solar system with large diverse groups of people by using existing resources from the planets, moons and asteroids.

(4) Give everyone the chance to lead a more personally fulfilling and socially responsible life.

(5) Leave the Sun behind entirely, sometime well before it burns out.

Artist's conception of terraforming Mars in four stages of development

(FIGURE 121) MARS TERRAFORM. DAEIN BALLARD

THE DISCOVERY OF LIFEPOINT

What if we find what we're looking for? What if we discover even a simple microorganism living in the soil on Mars?

Obviously this is not as dramatic as coming face to face with a bug-eyed alien walking on two legs, but discovering anything— a microbe, a plant, a bug—alive on another planet would cause a global epiphany: We are not alone! At that collective lifepoint, we would have to face the fact that the miracle of life reaches beyond Earth.

The discovery of life on another planet would be a major leap in humanity's self-awareness. The deep significance may not be immediately observable, but the discovery of other life could be the most important scientific enlightenment since Copernicus.

Everyday Travel Tip
BE A RESOURCEFUL TRAVELER

Whether traveling on-Earth or off-Earth, travel light and make the most of the resources at hand. A "live off the land" awareness inspires innovative and resourceful solutions that can help you thrive in your daily life. Reduce, reuse, recycle.

A small space colony on Mars could shield itself from solar radiation with Martian sediment and grow plants in biospheric greenhouses. (**FIGURE 122**) **MARS COLONY.** NASA

A LIFEPOINT OF COPERNICUS

In 1530, Copernicus (1473–1543) gave to the world his great work *De Revolutionibus*, which asserted a truth we now take for granted: that Earth rotated on its axis once daily and traveled around the Sun once yearly. This was a fantastic concept in a time when most people were fed the belief by religious leaders that humans were the center of the universe and superior to all other creatures. Copernicus carried on his celestial observations quietly and alone from a turret situated on the protective wall around the cathedral. His observations were made with bare eyes, as a hundred more years would pass before the invention of the telescope.

Copernicus died in 1543 and was never to know what a stir his work had caused. Two other Italian scientists of the time, and Giordano Bruno, even went beyond Copernicus.

NASA scientists have discovered a new form of microorganism living in California's toxic but exotic Mono Lake. As the water recedes, mineral deposits form strange towering spires, creating the perfect environment for the organism called *Spirochaeta americana*. (FIGURE 123) MONO LAKE. JOSEPH SOHM

Besides the Moon, Mars is the next closest celestial body humans may stand a chance of traveling to, and living on, in the foreseeable future. If the necessary resources are present, and we are smart enough to take advantage of them, human life may even thrive on the Red Planet.

Mars is a favorite focus for mankind. We've been going to Mars for 40 years. The first time we flew by another planet, it was Mars. The first time we orbited a planet, it was Mars. The first time we landed on and roved around the surface of another planet, it was Mars. (FIGURE 126) EARTH MARS UNIVERSE. NASA AND SPACE TRAVELER, INC.

In our every deliberation,
we must consider the impact
of our decisions on the next
seven generations.

———

THE GREAT LAW OF THE IROQUOIS CONFEDERACY
Dekanawida, Native-American
spiritual leader (1550 – 1600)

LIFE EXTENSION

I believe we as a species should take action to make the Drake equation factor "L"—the longevity of our "intelligent" civilization—as long an interval as possible. Learning to flourish on and off this planet will help ensure our collective survival.

Extending civilization will help us extend our own lives. The techniques being developed to stave off heart disease and cancer have the potential to halt or even reverse human aging. Stem cell research may one day repair broken spinal cords and grow replacements for tired hearts and lungs. Keeping people younger and healthier longer would also cut back on worldwide health spending and increase productivity.

"No one else can take care of your health except you," my dad used to say. If we take care of our health as best we can each day, we stand a better chance of benefiting from the next medical breakthroughs.

Photo of Iroquois people taken in 1914 at Buffalo, New York. The Iroquois believed that every action in the present had an impact on the next seven generations.

(Figure 127) 1914 Iroquois Native-American Group in Winter. Iroquois

Lance Armstrong beat cancer to become a seven-time Tour de France winner.
(FIGURE 128) LANCE ARMSTRONG.
ELIZABETH KREUTZ

LIVE STRONG AND THRIVE

The desire to do more than survive, to live and thrive, is common to all human beings. Deep down we all desire to be the heroes of our own lives.

At age 25, Lance Armstrong was one of the world's best cyclists. He proved it by winning race after race around the world. Lance Armstrong seemed invincible and his future was bright. Then they told him he had cancer.

During his treatment, before his recovery, before he even knew his own fate, he created the Lance Armstrong Foundation to help fight the disease.

Lance Armstrong beat his cancer and went on to become one of the world's greatest athletes. His seven Tour de France victories are awe-inspiring to sports fans, but his battle against cancer inspires millions of cancer survivors all around the world. Lance Armstrong is a shining example of the seventh insight in action: living strong and thriving.

Seventh Insight
LIVING TO THRIVE!

Live, love and laugh to the fullest but keep an eye toward the future. Like the Iroquois law says: your actions in the present affect seven generations to come. What can you do today that will make for a better tomorrow?

Be resourceful with what you have. Reduce, reuse and recycle.

The future is now. Thrive!

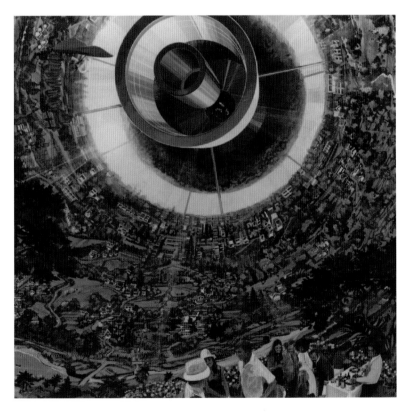

The people in the foreground of this painting are enjoying a day in their lives inside a Bernal sphere, one of several giant space colony designs explored by Gerard O'Neill in his landmark book *The High Frontier*.

(FIGURE 129) BERNAL SPHERE. DON DAVIS FOR NASA

Author's Log
NEW YEAR'S MORNING, JANUARY 1, 2101—PREPARING TO LEAVE

In longstanding naval tradition, the first entry of the new year is written in verse.

Today we launch for CosmicSea

and our journey back to Earth.

It's time to leave this other planet.

And return to the place of our birth.

The sunrise on Mars this morning was more beautiful than any I've seen since first landing on this incredible planet over a year ago. Just as the yellow sun broke on the orange horizon, an aura of reddish blue light glistened off wispy white clouds outside my MarsHab cabin window.

Usually I crawl out of my sleep sack and make a nice cup of coffee. But today I was so inspired, I didn't even make the coffee. I swallowed a coffee cube with some water and was out the hatch. Protected by my pressure suit that now smells like sweaty gym socks, I made my last trip to the rocky outcrop on the frozen spiral where we first found life on the surface of this strange but now familiar place.

In the past year, we've not only thrived in the enclosed biosphere of New Shangri-la, but we've explored the planet's polar regions and discovered a new form of life deep within the permafrost.

It's been a grand adventure, but we are all glad that the time has come to return home. We will miss our new friends, the inhabitants of New Shangri-la.

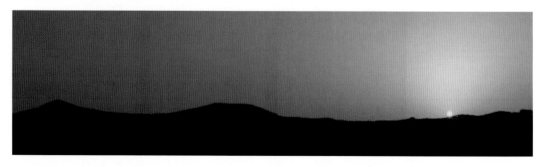

This is an actual color image of an actual sunset on Mars taken by *Pathfinder*. The two large mounds on the horizon are known as "Twin Peaks."

(FIGURE 130) MARS SUNSET. NASA

Two explorers search for life on Mars with the help of their robotic vehicle.
(FIGURE 131) EXPLORE MARS. DAVID A. HARDY/WWW.ASTROART.ORG

We also miss our families and friends on Earth. We long for their love and can't wait for their warm embraces.

We are proud to have helped a new offshoot of humanity take root on another planet. Our discovery of extraterrestrial life growing in the frozen spiral tundra of Mars will inspire an entire civilization with a grand new human realization.

We transmit this final message from an amazing planet where life strives to survive. Should something tragic happen on our way back home and these become the last words we transmit, know that we found something wonderful out here so far from home.

THERE IS LIFE ON ANOTHER PLANET—AND IT IS US!

We find ourselves pulled closer and closer to the black hole.

(Figure 132) Spiral Galaxy Ship. NASA and Space Traveler, Inc.

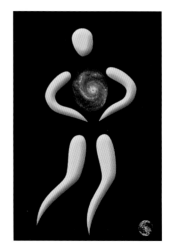

CHAPTER EIGHT

Embracing Mystery

Author's Log
HALFWAY HOME—THE IDES OF MARCH, 2101
INTO THE BLACK HOLE

Our journey back to Earth takes an unexpected and hypothetical detour through unexplored territory—the heart of the supermassive black hole in the center of our galaxy known as Sagittarius A*.

Sagittarius A* is 26,000 light-years away. Using current rocket systems, it would take generations of families living and dying on the same spacecraft for any one human to reach this distant but curious destination.

For our story, we'll have to bend reality. Imagine that an intense solar flare hits us like a rogue wave on the sea and sends us through a hyper-speed tunnel to the soul of our galaxy.

Within moments of being hit by the tsunami-sized wave of light, the three-mile-diameter black hole comes quickly into view. Suddenly, we find ourselves being pulled beyond its eerie edge of darkness into a spiraling free-fall. The force of the spin pins us against the walls of the vessel like the Tilt-a-Whirl ride in an amusement park. *CosmicSea* spirals wildly in a giant whirlpool of comets, planets and stars. Streaks of light flash outside the portholes.

Serenely let us move
to distant places
And let no sentiments
of home detain us.
The Cosmic Spirit seeks
not to restrain us
But lifts us stage by stage
to wider spaces.

Even the hour of
our death may send
Us speeding on to fresh
and newer spaces,
And life may summon us
to newer races.
So be it, heart:
bid farewell without end.

———
HERMANN HESSE, German-born Swiss writer
(1877 – 1962)

Anima alerts us, "We've lost control of our ship. The powers of the universe are in control. Go with the flow."

We proceed with caution into the unknown—but proceed we must. There is often something we need to see in what we don't understand.

How are we passing through the singularity of the black hole without being crushed and stretched into a single strand of atoms? What mystery lies at the bottom? What if there is no bottom to a black hole or an end to existence at all? What's happening to us?

Everything is growing deathly quiet as we spiral deeper into darkness, disappearing like water down a drain.

This is the view of our Milky Way's center when we stand on Earth at Zion National Park in Utah and look up into the night sky. The plane of the Milky Way's flat disk lies along the obvious band of clouds. The brightest white spot in the middle is the very center of the galaxy and marks the site of a supermassive black hole—Sagittarius A*. The black hole is concealed by the light from the stars and planets being sucked toward the event horizon that is only three miles in diameter.

(FIGURE 133) MILKY WAY ZION. WALLY PACHOLKA

It's not easy to see what our Milky Way Galaxy looks like since we live inside it. But it probably resembles the Whirlpool galaxy, a spiral galaxy similar to our own Milky Way. If we could take a comparable picture of the Milky Way, Earth would be in one of the outer arms of the spiral. (FIGURE 134) WHIRLPOOL M51. NASA

FOLLOW YOUR HEART AND MIND THROUGH MYSTERY

THIS LEG OF OUR JOURNEY TAKES US INTO the center of a supermassive black hole—one of the lingering mysteries of the universe. What lies inside the black hole's darkness: a giant incinerator or a wormhole to another place and time?

The universe itself is mysterious. We've all looked up at the countless stars in the night sky and asked ourselves the same questions that have inspired myths, religions and scientific inquiry for thousands of years. Why does the universe exist? What is my purpose in it? What happens after we die?

Some questions may simply never have answers. But if we use both our intellect and intuition, we can uncover many clues to nature's secrets and begin to solve the mysteries of the universe and the mysteries of our lives. Using our hearts and minds, we can apply nature's laws to create great art, solve crimes, discover medical breakthroughs and maybe someday peer into the mystery of a black hole.

Only one who will risk going too far can possibly find out how far one can go.

———

T.S. ELIOT, American-born English poet/ playwright (1888 – 1965)

INTO THE RABBIT HOLE

Black holes are basically invisible pits of gravity—a region of space crammed with so much matter that gravity becomes too strong for even light to escape. Whatever comes too close to the edge of a black hole, whether it's our spacecraft or a beam of light, will disappear like water spiraling down a drain. Once you go beyond the event horizon, you're going all the way.

At the very center of the black hole is a mystery scientists call "the singularity"—a point in space where all matter is crushed to infinite density and stretched into an infinitely long string of energy.

If you jumped into a black hole, you would begin to feel a sensation similar to when you stretch in the morning after getting out of bed. But ultimately the strength of the gravity becomes greater than the strength of the molecular bonds holding your flesh together.

You snap in two pieces, probably at the base of your spine. And then those two pieces snap in two. You go from one—to two—to four—to eight—to an infinite number of pieces. You become a long string of energy—like an endless piece of spaghetti. You would be what physicists call "spaghettified."

Do our pieces come out the other end? That has been the science fiction writer's dream—that if you fall into one side of a black hole you come out the other side. Some scientists believe a spacecraft like *CosmicSea* could travel intact through a supermassive black hole like the one at the center of our Milky Way Galaxy, 2.5 million times larger than our Sun. Here, the event horizon could be ten miles wide and we would experience only small effects of stretching and squeezing.

On the other hand, it's unlikely we would survive a trip through the smaller but more dangerous black hole formed from a highly compressed dying star with a mass so concentrated that it collapses in on itself. Earth would become such a tiny but powerful black hole if it were compressed to the size of a golf ball.

After almost 30 years of arguing that a black hole swallows up everything that falls into it, astrophysicist Stephen Hawking recently changed his view. The world-famous author of *A Brief History of Time* now says he and other scientists had gotten it wrong: black holes may in fact allow information to escape.

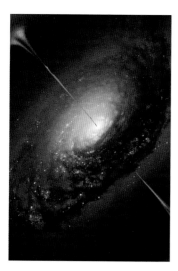

This altered image of Spiral Galaxy M64 depicts two infinite information streams entering a black hole between two points of the space-time continuum. (FIGURE 135) SPIRAL CONTINUUM. NASA AND SPACE TRAVELER, INC.

Hawking now says, "A black hole only appears to form, but later opens up and releases information about what fell inside. So we can be sure of the past and predict the future."[1]

Under his new theory, energy escapes from black holes in the form of photons, protons and other sub-atomic particles. If you fall into a black hole, the inventory of your particle composition—the information that makes you you—remains intact.

According to Einstein's famous equation $E=mc^2$—the recipe to exchange a quantity of matter with a quantity of energy and back again—the particle isn't crossing the event horizon and going into another universe. Instead, the energy field of a black hole appears to produce a counter particle based upon the information that comes in.

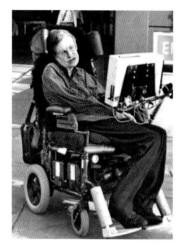

Professor Stephen Hawking
(Figure 136) Stephen Hawking.
Anonymous

In the same way, particles arise and disappear continuously in the empty space between planets, stars and galaxies—a place that isn't really empty at all but full of dark matter and zero-point energy. Wherever it is, it seems that space is being emptied at the same time it's being filled.

Stephen Hawking has been confined to a wheelchair most of his life due to Lou Gehrig's disease. But on April 26, 2007, Hawking took blissful leave of his wheelchair for a 90-minute airplane flight featuring 25-second bouts of weightlessness. "Life on Earth is at ever-increasing risk of being wiped out by a disaster, such as sudden global warming, nuclear war, a genetically engineered virus, or other dangers," he said in a statement. "I think the human race has no future if it doesn't go into space." (Figure 137) Hawking Zero G. Zero Gravity Corporation

SUPERSTRINGS AND THE COSMIC CONCERTO

Some scientists believe that the great mystery of black holes can be answered with the superstring theory—a "theory of everything" that attempts to explain the entire universe from the origin of the Big Bang down to the rose petals in a garden.

According to this holy grail of modern physics, vibrating one-dimensional "strings," not point-like particles, are the basic building blocks of reality. These tiny strings—about 100 billion times smaller than a proton—vibrate in four dimensions that we can observe and many other dimensions that we can't. What we see are the effects of a more complex reality in the same way the reflection of the Moon on a lake doesn't begin to explain the Moon itself. We can't always comprehend what we don't see.

Reality check: Just because you can't see something doesn't mean there isn't anything there. Imagine gazing at a TV set. We can easily comprehend the stories being told on the TV screen, yet the electronic wizardry inside the TV set is beyond most of our comprehension.

IN HARMONY WITH THE UNIVERSE

According to physicist and violinist Albert Einstein, a musical metaphor can help explain many great physical theories, including the superstring theory. Like the different strings on a guitar, superstrings have their own unique resonance or note. The different resonances of superstrings create the fundamental particles that we see, in the same way different finger positions on a guitar string create the specific notes that we hear.

The musical notes A, B, C, D, E, F and G that we create by pressing our finger down on the guitar string are not the critical part of the sound. What is fundamental is the guitar string itself. Without the guitar string, there would be no vibrations that create music.

Just as a vibrating guitar string produces various tones, a superstring vibrates in different frequencies, producing protons, neutrons, electrons or photons of light. According to these harmonic laws of physics, both our bodies and the entire universe can be described by the resonance of trillions of tiny strings. As the strings vibrate, they cause the surrounding space to shake. This symphony of vibrating superstrings harmoniously merges the microcosm of quantum mechanics with the macrocosm of the space-time continuum.

If we find the answer to why it is that we and the universe exist, it would be the ultimate triumph.

—

STEPHEN HAWKING, theoretical physicist and cosmologist (1942 –)

Albert Einstein riding a bicycle
(FIGURE 138) EINSTEIN BIKES.
ANONYMOUS

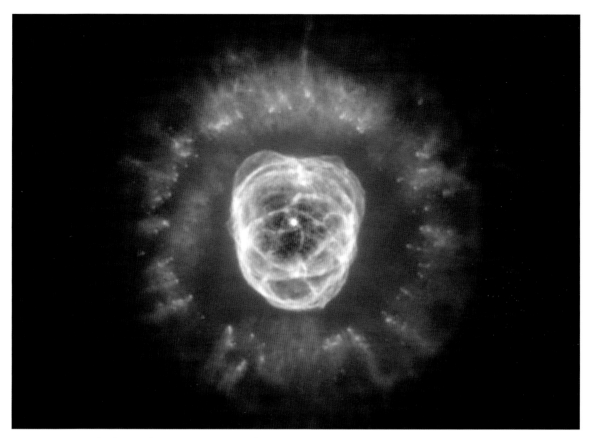

A superstring may look something like the interior of the Eskimo Nebula, but microscopic instead of macroscopic. The superstring theory may be the ultimate principle that Einstein died still trying to find. Superstrings may unify the micro-world of Einstein's quantum theory with his macro-world theory of general relativity.

(FIGURE 139) ESKIMO NEBULA. NASA/JPL

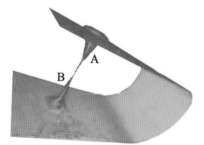

A graphic representation of the space-time continuum. Imagine folding a piece of paper over so that two points, A and B, almost touch. The distance traveling from point A to point B on the surface of the folded paper would be greater than if you could travel the space directly between the two points.

(FIGURE 140) SPACE-TIME. SPACE TRAVELER, INC.

THE GOLDEN SPIRAL

If we could jump into a black hole, we would be pulled toward the point of singularity, where the fabric of space-time tears and radically warps into a shape of infinite curvature. One possible shape of this infinite curving tunnel is known as the golden spiral, derived from a unique mathematical ratio that produces a series of infinitely smaller rectangles.

The golden spiral, first discovered by Pythagoras in the 5th century B.C., is one of the most intriguingly beautiful shapes found in nature: the Nautilus shell, the face of a sunflower, our fingerprints, our DNA, black holes and the shape of the Milky Way Galaxy we live in.

The spiral is evident in this picture of a hurricane taken from the International Space Station. (FIGURE 141) KATRINA. JEFF SCHMALTZ, MODIS RAPID RESPONSE TEAM, NASA/GSFC

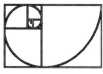  

The golden spiral contains a unique ratio that produces a series of infinitely smaller rectangles. (FIGURE 142) GOLDEN SPIRAL. SPACE TRAVELER, INC.

The nautilus shell, seen here in cross-section, possesses the golden spiral. (FIGURE 143) NAUTILUS SHELL. SPACE TRAVELER, INC.

The golden spiral can also be seen in this closeup of a sunflower plant. (FIGURE 144) SUNFLOWER. SPACE TRAVELER, INC.

Each of our one-of-a-kind fingerprints also contains this mysterious golden ratio… (FIGURE 145) FINGERPRINT. SPACE TRAVELER, INC.

…as does everyone's unique spiral of DNA. (FIGURE 146) DNA STRAND. SPACE TRAVELER, INC.

The golden spiral shows up not only in nature but also in art, music and other creations of beauty. Claude Debussy used it explicitly in his music and Le Corbusier in his architecture. There are claims that the golden ratio was used by Leonardo da Vinci in the painting of the *Mona Lisa*, by the Greeks in building the Parthenon and by ancient Egyptians in the construction of the Great Pyramid of Giza. Today, the use of the golden ratio in photography and other visual arts is known as the "rule of thirds."[2]

Even though mathematical truths like the golden ratio may help us understand black holes, what, if anything, really exists on the other side of this mysterious cosmic object? Are black holes a dead end or a doorway to another place and time?

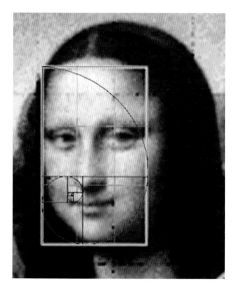

Leonardo da Vinci supposedly painted the *Mona Lisa* using the golden ratio, otherwise known as the rule of thirds. (FIGURE 147) *MONA LISA* MEME. SPACE TRAVELER, INC.

DEATH SPIRAL OR RE-CREATION?

Death is probably the greatest mystery that each of us must face. We have no proof that our "soul" either continues to exist after we die or simply disappears.

The Native Americans believe that when a person dies, their spirit still exists somewhere on Earth—in the sky, in the wind, in a flower or in space. Chief Seattle once said, "There is no death, only a change of worlds."

If our souls do exist and are not merely a product of our own bio-chemical minds, then what happens to us after we die? Perhaps death is merely a means for our souls to travel through the universe on a beam of light. The final mystery of any living creature may be what Welsh poet Alun Lewis calls, "the single poetic theme of life and death."

Every exit is an entry somewhere else.

———

Tom Stoppard,
playwright (1937 –)

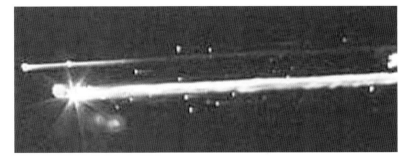

On February 1, 2003, the Space Shuttle *Columbia* STS-107 disintegrated upon re-entry, moments before its seven-member crew was scheduled to land in Florida. All seven astronauts died in the disaster. (**Figure 148**) *Columbia* Breaks Up. NASA

CLUES FROM YOUR HEART

Mystery is a vital part of life. Every day we are confronted with uncertainties with our work, our world and the people we love. Thriving in spite of these mysteries requires intuitive thinking—making daily decisions by "listening to our hearts."

As Albert Einstein once said, "The intuitive mind is a sacred gift and the rational mind is a faithful servant. There is no logical way to discover universal laws. There is only the way of intuition. The intellect has little to do on the road to discovery. There comes a leap in consciousness, call it intuition or what you will, the solution comes to you and you don't know how or why."

Such miracle discoveries occur when a scientist, on a hunch, squeezes a single drop of vaccine into a test tube and neutralizes a deadly virus. That one moment, driven by sheer intuition, can turn an instant into a historic moment that lasts forever and saves millions of lives. Miracles do happen.

The experience of space is what you make it. How deeply you penetrate its mysteries. How much you want to experience what is there.

————

STORY MUSGRAVE, astronaut/doctor
(1935 –)

Everyday Travel Tip
USE YOUR INTUITION

Spend a part of every day being creative. Whether it's music, art, writing, dance or woodworking, delve into the creative process on a daily basis. Turn a blank page into a work of art by listening to your heart.

The strong gravitational attraction between the two supermassive black holes in these two separate galaxies in the constellation of Canis Major is causing the formation of a brand-new single galaxy. (FIGURE 149) GALAXIES COLLIDE. SPACE TELESCOPE SCIENCE INSTITUTE/NASA/HUBBLE

WHAT'S LOVE GOT TO DO WITH IT?

Love may seem like a strange topic for a book about space travel. However, today's scientists talk about love, because their research demonstrates that disease is increased and longevity shortened by loneliness, isolation and depression. On the other hand, people who have strong bonds of love with others live longer and healthier lives. Love and compassion not only serve the greater good of society but also have a positive impact on our arteries, hearts and immune systems.

"Gravity and love are not that different," writes author Peter Russell.[3] Just as gravity is a force of attraction, so is love. Love is just a different kind of natural force.

Space travelers are human beings who need love. They have families, friends and pets back on Earth who love and miss them.

Like space travelers, most of us find comfort in knowing that someone loves us when we are far from home. In turn, we enjoy loving others—be it romantic, platonic or a love for your family or your country. Space travel inspires the higher aspect of love as defined by Russian actor Michael Chekhov, "a respect for all life— human, plant or animal."

SOMEWHERE OVER THE RAINBOW

Black holes are strangely beautiful objects. Yet what exists inside remains a mystery only because we have yet to invent a machine sophisticated enough to detect what's there.

Using our intellect, we've built electron microscopes that peer at the tiniest molecules of our makeup and developed powerful telescopes that see the immensity of distant galaxies. Yet the mystery of the black hole remains elusive.

Like burning wood becoming flame, isn't it possible that black holes may transform matter into a new reality that we can't currently perceive with our only human senses—sight, hearing, smell, taste and touch? Doesn't it seem plausible that the stars, planets and everything on them may be pulled into a black hole and recreated as something else—somewhere else?

"So what," you may say. "Why are black holes and superstrings important to me in my everyday life? Black holes don't help pay for my food and shelter." Maybe looking up at the night sky once in a while, toward the black hole at the center of our own Milky Way Galaxy, can shed insight into our daily lives, enriching each of us and the world as a whole.

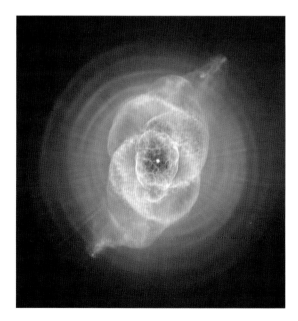

The dying star in the Cat's Eye Nebula throws off spirals of glowing gas. (FIGURE 150) CAT'S EYE NEBULA. NASA/HUBBLE

Tadpole Galaxy (FIGURE 151) TADPOLE GALAXY. NASA/HUBBLE

What if the universe explodes into existence not just once, but repeatedly in endless cycles of death and rebirth? Like a black hole, could it be that death carries our souls on the wings of superstrings through a golden spiral to be recreated as a star in someone else's sky, a flower in a distant garden or just another version of ourselves?

The answers to such questions remain mysteries. But what would life be without mystery?

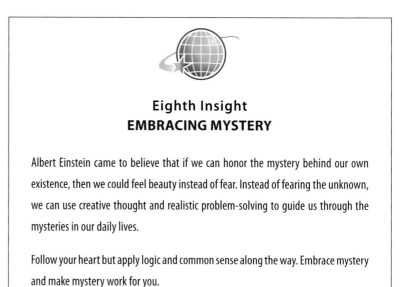

Eighth Insight
EMBRACING MYSTERY

Albert Einstein came to believe that if we can honor the mystery behind our own existence, then we could feel beauty instead of fear. Instead of fearing the unknown, we can use creative thought and realistic problem-solving to guide us through the mysteries in our daily lives.

Follow your heart but apply logic and common sense along the way. Embrace mystery and make mystery work for you.

What if we find life beneath the frozen, wind-blown golden spiral of Mars's North Pole?

(FIGURE 152) MARS NORTH POLE. NASA/JPL

Author's Log
PERSONAL AND CONFIDENTIAL—TIME UNKNOWN
SOMEWHERE AT THE EDGE OF MYSTERY

To my dearest Anna,

Maybe you'll never get this transmission. Our ship is spiraling out of control down a never-ending tunnel of darkness. Everyone else is unconscious—not dead, just in a deep sleep. I'm drifting off too.

I may not understand the mysteries of love but I do love you. I want to feel your comforting touch...to float weightlessly to you... our arms open...drawn together by the sheer gravity between our two bodies...our ultimate, timeless embrace.

This must be the reason the universe exists...to feel its own flesh against itself... through you and me...a moment to last forever...

Now I am so far away from you. Everything is dark, yet I can hear your voice, "Always come back. Come back to me."

If I'm to go anywhere when I die, let it be into your eyes.

(Computer Log: All systems are shutting down. Contact with mission control on Earth is now terminating.)

Michelangelo's Adam and Botticelli's Venus are spaghettified in a black hole.

(Figure 153) Venus-Adam. Michelangelo, Botticelli and Space Traveler, Inc.

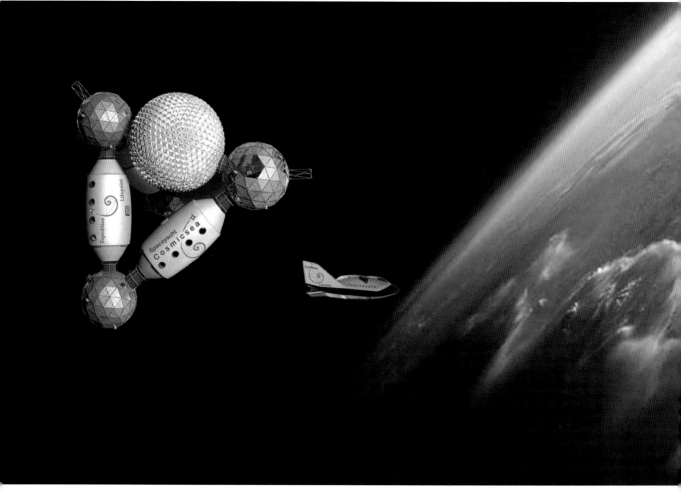

JourneyStar re-enters Earth's atmosphere.

(FIGURE 154) *JourneyStar* RETURNS. SPACE TRAVELER, INC.

CHAPTER NINE

Rediscovering Home

Author's Log
MAY 28, 2101—RETURNING HOME

Dazed but recovering from what feels like a long night's sleep, I float through the wheelhouse hatch and glide toward the helm. Over the ringing in my ears, I hear a faint familiar voice from Ground Control on the intercom, "Hello? *CosmicSea*, do you read me? Is anybody there?"

Fortunately we all survived our hypothetical journey through the black hole in the center of our galaxy. We've safely exited the other side of mystery and are now entering familiar territory.

There is no mistaking the welcoming hues of our home planet, slowly rotating outside *CosmicSea's* window. Below us we can sense wondrous life thriving in the green, blue, brown and white undulating across Earth's surface as if being painted before our eyes by the unseen hand of a great artist.

Happy but weary, we once again board *JourneyStar,* which has come to take us home. Once we're securely fastened in, a few powerful thruster blasts propel *JourneyStar* into the grasp of Mother Earth's gravity. As we enter the dense protective atmosphere, we shake in our seats like a roller coaster on steroids.

Much to our relief, the ship soon dives through a layer of clouds and levels out for landing. There is a clear view of the runway on the desert below. A large crowd of people have gathered to welcome us back.

We shall not cease
from exploration
And the end of all
our exploring
Will be to arrive
where we started
And know the place
for the first time.

———

T.S. Eliot, American-born English poet/ playwright (1888 – 1965)

Safe on the ground, we exit *JourneyStar* to a hero's welcome. With our first look around, we realize that the next part of our journey has only just begun.

We're not the same people who left many months ago. We're better because of our journey—but none of us could've imagined the changes that have happened here at home.

It may be that
the satisfaction I need
depends on
my going away,
so that when I've gone
and come back,
I'll find it at home.

———
RUMI, Persian philosopher
(1207 – 1273)

THERE'S NO PLACE LIKE HOME

LIKE DOROTHY IN *THE WIZARD OF OZ*, it feels good to be home after a long and harrowing journey. The extreme experiences we've had on our trip make us grateful for the familiar moments we find at home.

After floating weightless for months, we appreciate standing on firm ground. After breathing regenerated oxygen for so long, we relish our first breath of fresh Earth air. After living with the same small group of people on a daily basis, we cherish the hugs from loved ones we've long missed.

The Blue Marble is a spectacular true-color image of the entire Earth created from numerous satellite-based observations of the land, oceans, sea ice and clouds stitched together into a seamless mosaic including every square kilometer (.386 square mile) of our planet.

(FIGURE 155) BLUE MARBLE GLOBE. NASA

Mars over Poodle Rock, Nevada. In August 2003, Mars was as close to Earth as it had been in 59,619 years.
(FIGURE 156) MARS POODLE ROCK. WALLY PACHOLKA

On the MegaTransect expedition, conservationist Michael Fay set out to explore "the last place on Earth"—1,200 miles of untamed Africa—on foot. In the middle of his two-year trek through dense underbrush, deep mud, river crossings, malaria, foot worms, stick-hurling monkeys, elephants, gorillas and other rare animals, Michael felt the outside world would be foreign and hard to comprehend. Upon finally emerging onto the beaches of Gabon, he said, "I had tears in my eyes when I came back to a world I knew in the past."

When you're up there,
you know in your mind
that you are at the top rung
of the ladder of life.
What do you do
for an encore?

———

MIKE MULLANE, astronaut (1945 –)

What will we see when we rediscover home? Giant dirigibles, personal airplanes, solar-powered ships and automobiles? (FIGURE 158) FUTURESCAPE. SPACE TRAVELER, INC.

Upon our return to Earth, we discover a planet where men, women and children live and thrive among green landscapes, futuristic cities and happy, healthy Earthmates. In the space-traveler society, people go about their daily lives inside homes, schools and workplaces powered by sun, wind and water.

They travel to pyramid-shaped seaside resorts complete with ocean energy systems, fish farms, underwater hotels and human/dolphin encounters. They work in shimmering, solar-paneled buildings in cityscapes interlaced with miles-long wilderness greenbelts filled with once-endangered animals and plants. Entire desert communities thrive inside enormous clear geodesic domes housing a veritable oasis.

Overhead in clear blue skies, birds fly beneath sleek aircraft, floating dirigibles and elegant spaceships carrying passengers to orbit and beyond. At night, massive orbiting mirrors beam sunlight onto cities and farmland; their star-like glows form manmade constellations in space.

In the space-traveler society, human population remains at an optimal, sustainable size. We maximize the limitless amounts of energy from the Sun and halt the devastation of Earth.

Machines take over the mundane human tasks such as growing food and manufacturing products. As more of our needs are met without the exchange of currency or labor, we seek adventure, pleasure and deeply emotional experiences that become the stories of our lives.

Everyone's voice counts in our Internet-based democracy. Wealth is more evenly distributed. Far fewer people on the planet are hungry, homeless, helpless or hopeless.

The "Stanford Torus" design features a spinning outer ring that simulates gravity with centrifugal force. Centrifugal force is what keeps water in a pail when you swing it around your head. A 1/2-mile-diameter spinning structure could produce enough gentle gravity to give inhabitants an entertaining boardwalk where they can jog, stroll and socialize. (FIGURE 159) STANFORD TORUS. DON DAVIS FOR NASA

A colony like New Shangri-la could be built near Martian polar ice.

(FIGURE 160) MARS POLAR COLONY. DAVID A. HARDY/WWW.ASTROART.ORG

Crime, greed and power-hungry people still exist, but an evolved self-regulating society has created built-in checks and balances that enhance life for everyone. Philanthropy and generosity have become the standards to which most people strive. Love and romance evolve to higher levels, creating new kinds of families and friendships.

In the mature space-traveler society, millions of people live, work and play in space. Pilots fly us to orbiting hotels being built by space construction workers. Doctors and scientists discover breakthroughs in zero-gravity that cure disease and extend our lives. Paraplegics float about as freely as non-handicapped visitors. Vacationers enjoy recreational activities ranging from space sports to space sex.

Spacina, the first space marina, becomes an orbital gathering place for all kinds of space travelers, ranging from entrepreneurs looking for the next great opportunity to adventurers like you and me passing through this orbital outpost on our way to the Moon or Mars.

More and more people arrive on Mars and stay longer. They travel on large economical spacecraft and live in large greenhouses. These early pioneers make money by harvesting the valuable Martian isotope deuterium and shipping it back to Earth to produce trillions of dollars worth of power.

The Martian colonists begin the process of transforming Mars into a living, breathing, garden planet full of unique biomes and life forms. Eventually, children are born and raised on Mars. An offshoot of humanity takes root on the Red Planet.

Back on Earth, the space-traveler society fosters a new peace and prosperity unparalleled in the history of humankind.

This image of Earth's city lights maps the locations of permanent lights on the Earth's surface. The brightest areas are the most urbanized, but not necessarily the most populated. Cities tend to grow along coastlines and transportation networks. The United States Interstate Highway System appears as a lattice connecting the brighter dots of city centers. In Russia, the Trans-Siberian Railway is a thin line stretching from Moscow through the center of Asia to Vladivostok. The Nile River, from the Aswan Dam to the Mediterranean Sea, is another bright thread through an otherwise dark region.

(Figure 161) Earth-lit Night. Craig Mayhew and Robert Simmon, NASA/GSFC

CONCLUSION: PARTICIPATE IN LIFEPOINT

In every human life and in every civilization, there are turning points. These pivotal points in our personal lives may be of our own doing, such as graduating from school and getting married. But someone else or an act of nature may cause a turning point; a medical breakthrough can heal our lives, or a flash flood can destroy our homes. Such monumental moments radically change the way we act in the world.

Every day, each of us faces the ultimate turning point, a super paradigm, when life as we know it could end if we don't take action. Annihilation of life on Earth could come from a large meteor collision, a nuclear incident, a deadly virus or dramatic climate change.

Fortunately, we can **take part in the future by taking action in the present.** We live every day within nature's laws and principles. If we live every day as the space travelers we are, then each of us can not only survive but thrive in life. Who knows what lifepoints we may live to see?

Will it be a sudden, dramatic change in the environment, either man-made or natural, that wipes much of life off the planet? Or will it be a newfound prosperity for all life when human compassion, intelligence and foresight overcome greed, ignorance and shortsightedness?

As we've seen, the responses from people who have flown in space substantiate one basic premise: **the act of traveling in space can create profound changes in a person's life. People who travel to space will come to take for granted important insights that have taken those on Earth thousands of years to formulate.**

You must
be the change
you want to see
in the world.

——

GANDHI, Indian political and spiritual
leader (1869 – 1948)

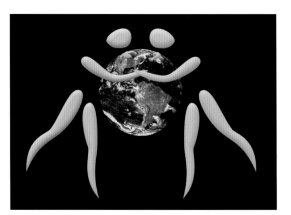

Participate in life.
(FIGURE 162) PARTICIPATE.
SPACE TRAVELER, INC.

Child of the Stars (FIGURE 163) STAR CHILD. NASA AND SPACE TRAVELER, INC.

Ed White, pilot of the Gemini 4 spaceflight, floats in the zero-gravity of space. This was
the first time an American stepped outside the confines of his spacecraft.

(Figure 164) Ed White. NASA/James McDivitt

The nine insights of space travelers are not magic incantations, spiritual dogma or surefire steps to success. They are simply nine aspects of surviving in space that can help each of us thrive on Earth every day.

NINE INSIGHTS OF SPACE TRAVELERS

1. **Space-Traveling Every Day:** "Know your surroundings" is the first law of survival. We are all shipmates on a singular planet in space and must work together to maximize our resources.

2. **Exploring Inner Space:** Remain calm. Let your inner strength guide you through the challenges in daily life.

3. **Experiencing Earthview:** Think differently. View your daily life from a new perspective.

4. **Feeling Weightless:** Sense those moments of weightlessness in between every step you take. Enjoy an attitude of lightness, and ease the sweet burdens of life.

5. **Connecting with the Biosphere:** Interplay with the web of life. Use your interconnectedness to all things to enhance your relationship with everyone and everything.

6. **Focusing on a Journeystar:** Navigate your life journey by triangulating your purpose, your proof and your passion so they converge on a single point of focus—a journeystar.

7. **Living to Thrive:** Do more than just survive; be resourceful with what you have. Reduce, reuse and recycle. Your actions in the present affect the future.

8. **Embracing Mystery:** Use logic and intuition to remain fearless in the face of the unknown. Creative thought and realistic problem-solving can guide you through the mysteries in your daily life. Make mystery work for you.

9. **Rediscovering Home:** Apply the wisdom from your journey to improve your daily life, your home and the world you live in.

Ninth Insight
REDISCOVERING HOME

Go on great adventures—but return home to discover the real treasures. We may search the solar system for other signs of life, but when we return home we appreciate the life we have even more.

Remember, the hero or heroine returns to everyday life with secret knowledge from distant domains and puts it to use in the redemption of society.

Participate in the unfolding drama of the universe every day. Become an active crewmember on spaceship Earth.

Milky Way over rock formation (FIGURE 165)
MILKY WAY ROCK HOLE. WALLY PACHOLKA

The Shellrock River in the summertime. Home at last. (FIGURE 166) SHELLROCK SUMMER. SPACE TRAVELER, INC.

Author's Log
FINAL ENTRY—THERE'S NO PLACE LIKE HOME

Expedition LifePoint may have come to an end,

but the rest of our journey lies ahead.

HAVE A GREAT ORBIT!

—SpaceJace

Deep space filled with billions of galaxies, each galaxy filled with billions of stars

(Figure 167) Deep Space Galaxies. NASA

The Next Adventure

IN THE 1936 MOTION PICTURE *Things to Come,* written by H.G. Wells, Sir Cedric Hardwicke's character raves at the head of his angry mob. He flails the air with his fist at man's first rocket to the Moon, poised on the launching pad. He cries out, "Cease! Desist! Turn back! We don't want mankind to go out to the Moon and the planets. We shall hate you more if you succeed than if you fail. Is there never to be calm and happiness for man?"

The radio transmits the captain's reply, "Either life goes forward or it goes back. Beware the concussion!"

In a huge telescope, the fathers of the two astronauts (a man and a woman) watch the flame of the spaceship moving toward the Moon. One says, "My God, is there never to be an age of happiness? Is there never to be rest?"

The other answers, "Rest enough for the individual man. Too much of it and too soon, and we call it death. But for man, no rest and no ending. He must go on—conquest beyond conquest. This little planet, its winds and waves, and all the laws of mind and matter that restrain him. Then the planets about him, and at last out across immensity to the stars. And when he has conquered all the deeps of space and all the mysteries of time, still he will be beginning."

He points out at the universe. "Is it that or this? All the universe—or nothingness. Which shall it be? Which shall it be?"

It's all perspective. What seems like the end may not be the end at all.

——

ANONYMOUS

Astronaut Buzz Aldrin, Apollo 11 Lunar Module pilot, deploys a solar wind experiment. In the background is the Lunar Module *Eagle*.

(Figure 168) Aldrin Experiments. NASA

Participate

HERE ARE SOME WAYS YOU CAN PERSONALLY GET
INVOLVED IN SPACE TRAVEL

PLAY YOUR PART

THE CURTAIN IS QUICKLY RISING on the grand stage of private space travel. Whether we realize it or not, we are all citizens of the new space-traveler society. Each of us can participate in creating this brave new world and share in the benefits space travel brings to our everyday lives.

Numerous organizations furthering space travel and a better future on Earth welcome your participation. The approaches may vary but the dream is the same. Simply type their names into any Internet search engine.

JOIN ORGANIZATIONS WHERE YOU CAN MEET PEOPLE WHO SHARE YOUR INTERESTS

If you're interested in bringing about radical breakthroughs for the benefit of humanity in the areas of education, exploration, energy and environment, check out the X-Prize website.[1]

If you like people in general, then check out organizations that deal with issues ranging from human psychology to philosophy and sexuality in space such as the Institute of Noetic Sciences,[2] founded by moonwalker Edgar Mitchell.

May the universe in some strange sense be brought into being by the participation of those who participate? The vital act is the act of participation. "Participator" is the incontrovertible new concept given by quantum mechanics.

———

JOHN WHEELER, American theoretical physicist (1911 – 2008)

If you like gardening or environmental issues, then you might want to explore organizations involved with biospheres, colonizing the Moon or terraforming Mars such as the Nature Conservancy, the World Wildlife Fund, the Mars Society[3] or the Artemis Project.[4]

If you like politics, then there are organizations like the National Space Society,[5] the Planetary Society,[6] the Space Frontier Foundation,[7] the Orange County Space Society (OCSS)[8] and the Space Foundation[9] that lobby for "space-friendly" laws and promote space awareness in the general public around the world. The Space Tourism Society,[10] founded by my long-time friend and associate John Spencer, would like to see space tourism available to as many people as possible, as soon as possible.

If your interests lie in the night sky and mysteries of our universe, check out the awesome pictures of the cosmos as seen by the great telescopes of our time: the Hubble Space Telescope,[11] the Spitzer Space Telescope[12] or the Chandra X-Ray Observatory.[13]

If you like art, there are organizations dedicated to depicting space creatively in music, words and the visual arts such as Novaspace[14] or SpaceArt.org.[15]

If you want to help your community in times of disaster, then join your local Citizen Corps.[16]

TALK ABOUT SPACE TRAVEL AND THE FUTURE

Whether you're talking to co-workers around the water cooler or neighbors in your local community, talk about how space travel can positively affect people's lives. Give a presentation at a local business gathering or your children's school. Nothing is better than the look in a child's eyes upon learning the wonders of the boundless space frontier that awaits her.

FINALLY, SUPPORT SPACE BUSINESSES AND ADVOCATES

Show your support by sending an email, or purchase some of the products they sell. Show them you believe in what they're doing.

Private space travel is helping to create a prosperous space-traveler society here on Earth. Join one of the greatest adventures of all humankind.

This is the last picture of our entire planet taken by a human being from space, during the Apollo 17 mission from a point halfway between Earth and the Moon. Because the Sun was directly behind the spacecraft, Earth appears fully illuminated. This has helped to make this photo the most commonly published photograph ever.

(FIGURE 169) EARTH-APOLLO 17. NASA

Acknowledgments

THIS STORY COULD ONLY BE TOLD with the help of many amazing people. I am deeply grateful to Anna Bogdanovich, my musical muse and mate for her passionate support along this journey, and to her brother, Peter Bogdanovich, for his insights into storytelling, film and poetry. I am equally indebted to my brother Jon who keeps me grounded in reality and to my mother and father for the awesome childhood they gave me along the magical Shellrock River.

I am especially thankful to my faithful companion on this creative quest, Dotti Albertine, who crafted the book's design and brought the images, words and adventure to life. Thanks also to Robin Quinn for editing the text to its essence, Brookes Nohlgren for putting her special editorial sparkle in the fine details, Flo Selfman for copyediting and to all the other editors for their comments, critiques and words of encouragement—Aileen Cho, Carol Givner and Jack Barnard.

My heartfelt gratitude goes out to everyone in the space-travel community—in particular, John Spencer, Tony Materna, Carlos Rocha and Charles Carr. These four dear friends and colleagues have explored space with me in many insightful conversations and fore-front design science projects.

I'm profoundly grateful to Buzz Aldrin, Story Musgrave and Rick Searfoss for sharing their space experiences with me personally, and to all the other brave astronauts for the insights they brought home. This acknowledgment must certainly include space tourism pioneers

Dennis Tito, Burt Rutan, Elon Musk, Richard Branson, Anousheh Ansari, Jeff Bezos, Robert Bigelow, Eric Anderson and Peter Diamandis, among others, for making private space travel possible.

I also want to express my appreciation to the leaders, visionaries and storytellers who inspire all of us with the excitement and promise of space travel—George Lucas, James Cameron, Ron Howard, Tom Hanks, Lou Dobbs, Miles O'Brien, Rick Tumlinson, George Whiteside, Loretta Hidalgo, Michelle Evans, Lori Garver, Robert Zubrin, Neil deGrasse Tyson, Ray Bradbury and many others.

I wish to thank *all* my courageous companions on this voyage of discovery, whose own remarkable journeys have fortunately intertwined with mine. These shipmates include America's photographer Joe Sohm, Greg Snegoff, Dan Cohen, Steve Beckwith, Peter Russell, Jeff Hutner, Paul Roth, John Berwick and David Neale, to name a few; and to all my childhood friends along the bucolic Shellrock River. It's such a pleasure traveling with each of you on this magnificent spaceship Earth.

Notes

INTRODUCTION | WHY GO?

1 White, Frank. Paraphrased from his book, *The Overview Effect*. American Institute of Aeronautics and Astronautics, 1977, 1998.

2 Gladwell, Malcolm. *The Tipping Point*. Little, Brown and Company, 2000.

3 Vinge, Vernor. *The Whole Earth Review*, Winter 1993.

4 Russell, Peter. *Waking Up in Time*. Origin Press, Inc., 1998.

CHAPTER 1

1 People at the equator rotate on the Earth's surface faster than anywhere else on the planet—slightly over 1,000 miles per hour.

2 Schmitt, Harrison "Jack." From an article by Paul Hoversten, Washington Bureau chief, posted April 24, 2000, on www.Space.com.

3 Beebe, William. *Half Mile Down*. Duell, Sloan and Pearce, 1962.

CHAPTER 2

1 Among those attending were Dennis Tito, John Spencer, Tony Materna, Charles Carr, Larry Evans, Hank Murdock and the author.

2 Grosso, Michael. *Essay from Voices on the Threshold of Tomorrow*. Quest Books, 1993.

3 Buckey, Jay. Dartmouth University. From the article "Can We Go to Mars Without Going Crazy?" *Discover Magazine*, May 2001.

4 Wood, JoAnna. Chief research scientist at OPS-Alaska, an extreme environments research firm. *Discover Magazine*, May 2001.

5 Aldrin, Buzz. Quoted in the *Los Angeles Times* article "Making It" by Susan Vaughn, January 28, 2001.

CHAPTER 3

1 White, Frank. *The Overview Effect, Space Exploration and Human Evolution*. American Institute of Aeronautics and Astronautics, 1998.

2 Paraphrased from Skylab astronaut Ed Gibson in the book by Frank White, *The Overview Effect*, American Institute of Aeronautics and Astronautics, 1998.

CHAPTER 4

1 Any object in free-fall experiences microgravity conditions, which occur when the object falls toward Earth with an acceleration equal to that of gravity alone (approximately 9.8 meters per second squared [m/s^2], or 1 G at Earth's surface).

2 Fuller, Buckminster. *Critical Path*. St. Martins Press, 1981.

3 Lucid, Shannon. NASA Habitation Module Commercialization Conference. August, 1999.

4 Chekhov, Michael. *To the Actor*. Harper Collins, 1953.

5 Kustenmacher, Werner. *The Moon: A Guide for First-time Visitors* (Frommer's). Macmillan, 1999.

CHAPTER 5

1 Lovelock, James. *Healing Gaia*. Harmony Books, 1991.

2 Capra, Fritjof; Steindl-Rast, David; Matus, Thomas. *Belonging to the Universe*. San Francisco: Harper & Row, 1991.

3 Gelb, Michael J. *How to Think Like Leonardo da Vinci*. Delacorte Press, 1998.

4 Perron, Richard. Recounting from Dr. Bombard's log notes. *The Survival Bible*. 2001.

5 Wiseman, John "Lofty." *The SAS Survival Handbook*. Harper Collins, 1986.

6 Watts and Strogatz report in *Nature Magazine*, vol. 393, p. 440, 2006.

7 Shepanek, Marc. From "Can We Go to Mars Without Going Crazy?" by William Speed Weed. *Discover Magazine*, May 2001.

CHAPTER 6

1 Wiseman, John "Lofty." *The SAS Survival Handbook*. Harper Collins, 1986.

2 A common misconception is that solar sails are pushed by the solar wind just as sailboats are propelled by the wind on Earth. This is not so. The solar wind is an extremely tenuous flow of particles streaming away from the Sun. It exerts very little force on anything it hits. The propulsive force for a solar sail arises from the pressure of photons (light) from the Sun or potentially from lasers. Sunlight at 1 astronomical unit (1 AU is Earth's distance from the Sun—approximately 150 million kilometers or 93 million miles) exerts a force of 9 Newtons per square kilometer (0.78 pounds per square mile) on a solar sail.

3 Zubrin, Robert, and Richard Wagner. *The Case for Mars*. Touchstone, 1996. Robert Zubrin believes the best trajectories between Earth and Mars for a piloted Mars mission are those that leave Earth with a departure velocity of 5.08 km/s and leave Mars with a departure velocity of about 4 km/s. At these speeds, time to Earth return is 2 years. Transit time to Mars is 180 days and safe aero-braking into Mars's orbit is possible.

CHAPTER 7

1 Bradbury, Ray. Paraphrased from a 1981 *Reader's Digest* article and one of the several times I heard Bradbury tell this story in person.

2 Drake, Frank. Drake is an astronomer with the Search for Extraterrestrial Intelligence Institute, commonly known as SETI. Drake developed a theoretical tool for calculating the number of planets with civilizations advanced enough to broadcast signals within radio range of SETI's large satellite dishes on Earth. The Drake equation, $n = r^* f_p n_e f_l f_i f_c l$, is easy to understand.

R^* tells us the number of stars in our galaxy within radio range of the large satellite dishes searching for them, an area approximately 100 billion stars wide. The factor f_p is the fraction of those stars with planets—a number we are getting a better understanding of with the discovery of more planets in nearby solar systems. Factor n_e is the number of planets that could support life. The fourth factor, f_l, is the number of planets that actually do harbor life.

The next factor, f_i, tells us the number of planets where life developed intelligence. Drake's f_c factor identifies the number of planets with creatures that can communicate by sending radio signals and transmitting information.

The final factor, l, represents the longevity of "intelligent" civilizations. L tells us the number of years the technology of intelligent civilizations has been emitting radio signals. Modern humans have been broadcasting radio signals less than a hundred years. We've been on Earth such a short amount of time that it's not yet clear that a brain like ours is necessarily a long-term advantage.

3 Davies, Paul. *The Fifth Miracle.* Physicist Paul Davies makes a case for the exchange of life between Mars and Earth. Simon & Schuster, 1999.

4 McKay, Christopher P. From the article, "Bringing Life to Mars." *Scientific American Presents the Future of Space Exploration Quarterly.* May, 1999.

5 Menkhoff, Nicole. Embry-Riddle Aeronautical University. Menkhoff writes: "The industry of tomorrow and the students of today share a common interest. To them, living and working on Mars does not sound like science fiction, it sounds like the future."

CHAPTER 8

1 Hawking, Stephen. According to the online article "Hawking Loses Bet; Changes Mind on Black Holes" by Jane Wardell, Associated Press, British Broadcasting Corporation's "Newsnight" program, posted 06:53 am ET, 16 July 2004.

2 The appeal of the golden ratio to the human eye and brain has been scientifically proven ever since the first tests done by German physicist Gustav Fechner in the 1860s.

3 Russell, Peter. *Waking Up in Time.* Origin Press, Inc., 1998.

CHAPTER 9

1 Houston, Jean. "Living in One's and Future Myths" from *Fabric of the Future* edited by M.J. Ryan. Conari Press, 1998.

PARTICIPATE

1 X Prize Foundation. www.x-prize.org

2 Institute of Noetic Sciences. www.noetic.org

3 The International Mars Society. www.marssociety.org

4 Artemis Society. www.asi.org

5 National Space Society. www.nss.org

6 The Planetary Society. www.planetary.org

7 The Space Frontier Foundation. www.spacefrontier.org

8 Orange County Space Society. www.ocspace.org

9 Space Foundation. www.spacefoundation.org

10 Space Tourism Society. www.spacetourismsociety.org

11 Hubble Space Telescope. www.hubblesite.org

12 Spitzer Space Telescope. www.spitzer.Caltech.edu

13 Chandra X-Ray Observatory. www.chandra.harvard.edu

14 Novaspace. www.novaspace.com

15 SpaceArt.org. www.spaceart.org

16 Citizen Corps. www.citizencorps.gov

Credits

All photographs and illustrations copyright by their respective sources. Every effort has been made to trace and credit the copyright holders, but in case of error, the publisher will be happy to amend credits in future editions.

1. Book cover. Space Traveler, Inc.
2. Shellrock Winter. Space Traveler, Inc.
3. EVAtion. NASA
4. Stellar Spire. NASA, ESA and The Hubble Heritage Team (STScI/AURA)
5. Tito. ITAR-TASS
6. *SpaceShipOne* and *White Knight*. Mojave Aerospace Ventures, LLC.
7. *SpaceShipOne* Apex. Mojave Aerospace Ventures, LLC.
8. *SpaceShipOne* Returns to Earth. Mojave Aerospace Ventures, LLC.
9. Mike Mullane. NASA/Johnson Space Center
10. Expedition LifePoint. Space Traveler, Inc.
11. Videotron. Space Traveler, Inc.
12. *CosmicSea* Departs. Space Traveler, Inc.
13. Weightless. Space Traveler, Inc.
14. Mars Explorers. NASA/JSC by Pat Rowlings
15. Ed Gibson. NASA/Marshall Space Flight Center
16. Tipping Point. Space Traveler, Inc.
17. de Chardin. Anonymous
18. LifePoint Cliff. Space Traveler, Inc.
19. Blue Marble West. NASA
20. Spacewalking MMU. NASA
21. Ed White. NASA
22. Weightless Child. Copyright Joseph Sohm/ visionsofamerica.com
23. Parabolic. Space Traveler, Inc.
24. Parabolic-Play. NASA
25. Everest. NASA
26. Beebe. Wildlife Conservation Society
27. OTEC Installation. Space Traveler, Inc.
28. *Genesis 2*. Bigelow Aerospace
29. Eclipse. NASA
30. Pyramid Moon. Space Traveler, Inc.
31. Alan Bean. NASA
32. Thinker. NASA and Space Traveler, Inc.
33. Edgar Mitchell. NASA and Space Traveler, Inc.
34. Helms-Voss. NASA
35. Animasphere-Helms. NASA and Space Traveler, Inc.
36. Apollo 13. NASA
37. Apollo 13 Repair. NASA
38. Big Impact. Don Davis for NASA
39. Buzz Aldrin. NASA
40. Eye Storm. Space Traveler, Inc.
41. Earth Water. NASA
42. SAFER Rescue. NASA/JSC

43. Face-in-*Mir*. NASA
44. *Kon-Tiki*. Anonymous
45. Inner Space Shore. Space Traveler, Inc., and Jon Klassi
46. Dolphin. Space Traveler, Inc.
47. Earthview Flare. NASA
48. Tiny Blue Dot. NASA
49. Apollo 8 View. NASA
50. Earthrise. NASA
51. *SpaceShipOne* Separates. Scaled Composites/ Mike Masse
52. Gulf of Mexico. The SeaWiFS Project, NASA/ Goddard Space Flight Center and ORBIMAGE
53. Sunrise. NASA
54. First Spacewalk. NASA
55. Saint-Exupéry. Clete Delvaux
56. Earth Pool Ball. NASA
57. *JourneyStar* Arrives. Space Traveler, Inc.
58. Weightless Plane. NASA
59. Anousheh Ansari. Copyright © 2007 Prodea Systems, Inc. All rights reserved. Used under permission of Prodea Systems, Inc.
60. Newton Cannonball. Space Traveler, Inc.
61. Skylab Astrobats. NASA
62. Free-falling. NASA/JSC
63. MMU Close-up. NASA
64. HSA Diver. Handicapped Scuba Association
65. GeoDome. Space Traveler, Inc.
66. Allende Meteorite. D. Ball, ASU
67. *CosmicSea* Napkin. Space Traveler, Inc.
68. *CosmicSea* Rear. Space Traveler, Inc.
69. Animasphere-ISS. NASA and Space Traveler, Inc.
70. Valentina Tereshkova. Associated Press
71. Sally Ride. NASA
72. Christa McAuliffe. NASA
73. Shannon Lucid. NASA
74. Cosmic Sutra. Space Traveler, Inc.
75. Bacchante. Copyright © 2005 Daniel P. B. Smith and released under the terms of the GFDL
76. Story Musgrave. Story Musgrave
77. CabinHab View. Space Traveler, Inc.
78. *CosmicSea* Orbits. Space Traveler, Inc.
79. Bluebio. NASA
80. Ecosphere. Ecosphere Associates, Inc.
81. CELSS. NASA
82. Stanford Torus. NASA
83. Exosphere Inside. Space Traveler, Inc.
84. Quinoa Plant. Anonymous
85. Quinoa Pilaf. Space Traveler, Inc.
86. Biosphere 2. Gill Kenny, reprinted with permission of Global Ecotechnics
87. Ocean View. NASA
88. Bombard. *Mon Journal*
89. Six Degrees. Space Traveler, Inc.
90. Ripple Effect. "Juggling"—Copyright © 2006, Martin Waugh, www.liquidsculpture.com
91. ISS STS-107 Crew. NASA
92. Biosphere Port. Space Traveler, Inc.
93. Your Web. Space Traveler, Inc.
94. *CosmicSea* Leaves. Space Traveler, Inc.
95. Renaissance Man. Anonymous
96. Radio Telescope. Jet Propulsion Laboratory
97. Triangulation. Space Traveler, Inc.
98. North Star. Wally Pacholka
99. North Star Chart. NASA and Space Traveler, Inc.
100. Kepler. Artist Unknown
101. Lightcraft. Rensselaer Polytechnic Institute, White Sands, New Mexico
102. *CosmicSea* Sails. NASA/Planetary Society and Space Traveler, Inc.
103. Aurora. European Space Agency
104. *CosmicSea* Retros. Space Traveler, Inc,
105. *LifeLander*. Space Traveler, Inc.
106. *LifeLander*. Chute. NASA and Space Traveler, Inc.
107. New Shangri-la. Space Traveler, Inc.
108. Mars Frost. NASA/JPL
109. Mars Clouds. NASA/JPL
110. First Landing. NASA
111. Olympus Mons. NASA/JPL
112. Olympus Mons Side. NASA/JPL
113. Mars Ocean. NASA Mars Global Surveyor Project; MOLA Team. Rendering by Peter Neivert, Brown University
114. New Shangri-la Site. NASA and Space Traveler, Inc.
115. Manta Ray. Rainbow Divers
116. Jellyfish. Steve Clabuesch, National Science Foundation
117. *War of the Worlds*. George Pal

118. Europa. NASA
119. Deep Space. NASA/ESA
120. Tsiolkovsky. CPA/USSR
121. Mars Terraform. Daein Ballard
122. Mars Colony. NASA
123. Mono Lake. Joseph Sohm
124. Copernicus. Anonymous
125. Mono Lake Life. NASA/NSSTC
126. Earth Mars Universe. NASA and Space Traveler, Inc.
127. 1914 Iroquois Native-American Group in Winter. Iroquois
128. Lance Armstrong. Elizabeth Kreutz
129. Bernal Sphere. Don Davis for NASA
130. Mars Sunset. NASA
131. Explore Mars. David A. Hardy/www.astroart.org
132. Spiral Galaxy Ship. NASA and Space Traveler, Inc.
133. Milky Way Zion. Wally Pacholka
134. Whirlpool M51. NASA
135. Spiral Continuum. NASA and Space Traveler, Inc.
136. Stephen Hawking. Anonymous
137. Hawking Zero G. Zero Gravity Corporation
138. Einstein Bikes. Anonymous
139. Eskimo Nebula. NASA/JPL
140. Space-time. Space Traveler, Inc.
141. Katrina. Jeff Schmaltz, MODIS Rapid Response Team, NASA/GSFC
142. Golden Spiral. Space Traveler, Inc.
143. Nautilus Shell. Space Traveler, Inc.
144. Sunflower. Space Traveler, Inc.
145. Fingerprint. Space Traveler, Inc.
146. NA Strand. Space Traveler, Inc.
147. *Mona Lisa* Meme. Space Traveler, Inc.
148. *Columbia* Breaks Up. NASA
149. Galaxies Collide. Space Telescope Science Institute/NASA/Hubble
150. Cat's Eye Nebula NASA/Hubble
151. Tadpole Galaxy. NASA/Hubble
152. Mars North Pole. NASA/JPL
153. Venus-Adam. Michelangelo, Botticelli and Space Traveler, Inc.
154. *JourneyStar* Returns. Space Traveler, Inc.
155. Blue Marble Globe. NASA
156. Mars Poodle Rock. Wally Pacholka
157. Cave Creation. Space Traveler, Inc.
158. Futurescape. Space Traveler, Inc.
159. Stanford Torus. Don Davis for NASA
160. Mars Polar Colony. David A. Hardy/www.astroart.org
161. Earth-lit Night. Craig Mayhew and Robert Simmon, NASA/GSFC
162. Participate. Space Traveler, Inc.
163. Star Child. NASA and Space Traveler, Inc.
164. Ed White. NASA/James McDivitt
165. Milk Way Rock Hole. Wally Pacholka
166. Shellrock Summer. Space Traveler, Inc.
167. Deep Space Galaxies. NASA
168. Aldrin Experiments. NASA
169. Earth-Apollo 17. NASA

Index